D1321502

Hugh Westacott was born in London in 1932 and moved to Epsom, Surrey, on the outbreak of the war. He was educated at Tiffin Boys' School, Kingston-upon-Thames, and the North-Western Polytechnic. He was for ten years the Deputy County Librarian of Buckinghamshire and has also worked as a librarian in Sutton, Croydon, Sheffield, Bradford and Brookline, Massachusetts. During the war he spent his holidays with his family in Colyton, east Devon, walking five miles to the sea and back again each day, and his love of walking stems from these experiences. He is now a freelance writer and lecturer and in 1979 he was commissioned by Penguin to write this series of footpath guides to every national park and official long-distance path. He has also written *The Walker's Handbook* (Penguin, second edition 1980) and two forthcoming books, *Long-Distance Paths: An International Directory* and *The Backpacker's Bible*. His other interests include the history of the Royal Navy in the eighteenth century and the writings of Evelyn Waugh. Hugh Westacott is married and has two daughters.

Mark Richards was born in 1949 in Chipping Norton, Oxfordshire. He was educated at Burford Grammar School before training for a farming career. He discovered the pleasures of hill walking through a local mountaineering club. He became friends with Alfred Wainwright, the creator of a unique series of pictorial guides to the fells of northern England, who encouraged him to produce a guide to the Cotswold Way, which was followed by guides to the North Cornish Coast Path and Offa's Dyke Path. For two years he produced a selection of hill walks for the *Climber and Rambler* magazine, and more recently he has contributed articles and illustrations to the *Great Outdoors* magazine and numerous walking books, culminating in the present series of Penguin footpath guides. As a member of various conservation organizations and a voluntary warden of the Cotswolds Area of Outstanding Natural Beauty, he is interested in communicating the need for the protection of environmental and community characteristics, particularly in rural areas. Mark Richards is happily married with two lively children, Alison and Daniel.

The Penguin Footpath Guides

To be published:

Already published:

The North Downs Way

H. D. Westacott

With maps by Mark Richards

Penguin Books

This guide is dedicated with love and gratitude to the memory of my father, Charles Douglas Westacott (1902–82) of Godalming, Surrey. He loved the British countryside and was particularly fond of walking on the North Downs

Penguin Books Ltd, Harmondsworth, Middlesex, England
Penguin Books, 625 Madison Avenue, New York, New York 10022, U.S.A.
Penguin Books Australia Ltd, Ringwood, Victoria, Australia
Penguin Books Canada Ltd, 2801 John Street, Markham, Ontario, Canada L3R 1B4
Penguin Books (N.Z.) Ltd, 182–190 Wairau Road, Auckland 10, New Zealand

First published 1983

Made and printed in Great Britain by
Richard Clay (The Chaucer Press) Ltd, Bungay, Suffolk
Filmset in Monophoto Univers by
Northumberland Press Ltd, Gateshead

Contents

Acknowledgements

I should like to express my appreciation for the help given by the Countryside Commission and Kent County Council in the preparation of this guide.

As always, a great debt of gratitude is owed to Mark Richards, who drew the superb maps which contribute so much to the guide, and also to Sue Baylis, who typed the manuscript.

The maps are based on the Ordnance Survey maps with the sanction of the Controller of Her Majesty's Stationery Office (Crown copyright reserved).

Introduction

The North Downs Way (long-distance path B1) runs from Farnham in Surrey to Dover in Kent, via Boughton Aluph and Folkestone, for a distance of 124 miles. From Boughton Aluph to Dover there is an alternative route via Canterbury. If this route is chosen the distance from Farnham to Dover is 131 miles. Some walkers like to turn the alternative sections from Boughton Aluph into a circular walk so that they finish there rather than at Dover, which makes the total distance about 156 miles. In this guide the shorter route via Folkestone is regarded as the main route and the miles indicated on the map run consecutively from Boughton Aluph via Folkestone to Dover. The alternative route via Canterbury is treated in exactly the same way as the main route except that after Boughton Aluph the miles are measured from 1 again. The miles are used both on the maps and in the text to identify places quickly, so walkers should note that in the text miles between Boughton Aluph and Dover via Canterbury are prefixed with C (for Canterbury). This section of the Path will be found on pp. 118–41.

The North Downs Way was designated a long-distance path by the Countryside Commission, which, with the County Councils of Kent and Surrey, has overall responsibility for the Path. It was opened in 1978 by the Archbishop of Canterbury. There are one or two short stretches of the route which at present follow roads or alternative paths because rights of way along the official route have not yet been negotiated with the landowners. Such diversions from the official route are noted in the text and both the temporary and permanent routes are shown on the maps. The final route should not be used until such time as signposts and waymarks indicate that it is open.

The North Downs Way was created to take advantage of the natural beauty of the chalk downs which stretch from Farnham to Dover and also because it follows the general line of the ancient trackway known as the Pilgrims' Way. For the whole of its length the path passes through the North Downs Area of Outstanding Natural Beauty, although the alternative route via Canterbury leaves the designated area. When compared with the

South-West Peninsula Coast Path, the Cleveland Way and the Pennine Way, the scenery is not spectacular, but it is extremely attractive, there are many delightful towns, villages and places of historical interest along the route and there are often quite extensive views.

The North Downs Way crosses the southern side of London – at one point it is less than 20 miles from Hyde Park Corner – and it also brushes the edge of the Medway towns. It passes through many towns of some size and the whole route is through the densely populated corner of south-east England, much of it commuter country. It can be surprisingly rural, but the wayfarer will often be conscious of the dull roar of distant traffic pouring along the main roads parallel to the Path.

Long-distance paths were established for pleasure, not for record-breaking purposes. Because our lives are governed by the need to conserve time, there is an unfortunate tendency to try to walk the route as quickly as possible. Unless you derive particular pleasure from testing yourself to the limit, take plenty of time and savour every moment of the walk. It is better to be able to laze in the sun after a pleasant lunch, to explore some of the attractive towns and villages along the route, to watch the wild life and to examine the flowers than to have the nagging urge to keep going in order to keep to a tight schedule. Those who have walked long-distance paths know what Robert Louis Stevenson meant when he wrote, 'To travel hopefully is a better thing than to arrive.'

As long-distance paths go, the North Downs Way is an easy walk, the significant hills are few and the gradients rarely steep, so that it makes an ideal introduction to the pleasures of long-distance walking. It is particularly suitable for young people seeking their first taste of adventure. Public transport is exceptionally good and it is easy to walk the route in a series of separate day trips (see p. 9).

Many people walk the North Downs Way in the course of a year and if its charm and beauty is to be preserved it is incumbent upon everyone to avoid polluting it and thus making it unpleasant for those who follow. Never on any account drop litter or light a fire. All litter should be carried in a plastic bag until it can be deposited properly in a litter bin. Do not hide it behind a convenient bush, because out of sight is not always out of mind, and that hidden plastic bag may be swallowed by farm animals or a favourite pony, possibly with fatal results. Tin cans can cause serious injuries to livestock. When nature calls, retire modestly into some protective bushes, scrape a shallow pit with the heel of your boot or with a stick and cover the stools and toilet tissue with a sprinkling of soil. If all Britons would obey the instructions contained in the country code which have been preached at them for many, many years we would soon lose the reputation of living in the dirtiest country in Europe.

Enjoy the countryside and respect its life and work.
Guard against all risk of fire.
Fasten all gates.
Keep dogs under close control.
Keep to public paths across farmland.
Use gates and stiles to cross fences, hedges and walls.
Leave livestock, crops and machinery alone.
Take your litter home.
Help to keep all water clean.
Protect wild life, plants and trees.
Take special care on country roads.
Make no unnecessary noise.

Planning the walk

When planning a walk along any long-distance path, the walker has to make two decisions which will affect the course of all his future actions. The first decision is in which direction to walk the path. The second is whether he will walk it in consecutive days or make a series of single-day excursions. Direction is a matter of personal preference. Most people seem to walk from west to east (Farnham to Dover), which means that they have the prevailing wind behind them, and I suppose some people will enjoy the sensation of walking to the very edge of Britain and seeing France and the Continent across the straits of Dover.

Walkers who prefer to walk the North Downs Way in a series of separate day excursions will find that this is easier than on any other long-distance path. There is an extensive rail network into London crossing the Path at frequent intervals and there is a line which runs parallel to the Path on an east–west axis.

Public transport

In order to plan the walk in a series of stages it will be necessary to consult bus and rail timetables. Some information about transport services will be found in the text, but of necessity it is brief and does not include timetables. Preference in the list of destinations is given to stops along the line of the path. Rail timetables for the whole country are published in one volume and may be consulted at any railway station and in most public libraries. Bus timetables are more difficult to refer to outside the area which they serve, but they may be purchased by post from the relevant bus company. The following bus timetables cover the whole route:

Guildford and Woking (Area 6)
East Surrey (Area 5)
Sevenoaks (Area 3)
Gravesend, Dartford and Swanley (Area 2)

published by and available from London Country Bus Services Ltd, Lesbourne Road, Reigate, Surrey RH2 7LE (tel. (07372) 42411).

Maidstone (Area 1)
Medway (Area 3)
Canterbury (Area 5)
Dover (Area 7)
Shepway (Area 8)
Ashford (Area 9)

published by and available from East Kent, Maidstone and District Services Ltd, Bus Station, Canterbury CT1 2SY (tel. (0227) 63482).

The following is a list of railway stations which lie within two miles of the North Downs Way. The approximate distance from the Path is indicated together with the nearest mile point shown on the map.

Farnham: on Path
Shalford: 1 mile at mile 11
Guildford: $\frac{1}{2}$ mile at mile 11
Chilworth: 1 mile at mile 13
Gomshall and Shere: 1 mile at mile 17
Dorking Town: $\frac{1}{2}$ mile at mile 22
Dorking North: $\frac{1}{2}$ mile at mile 23
Deepdene: 1 mile at mile 23
Box Hill: $\frac{1}{4}$ mile at mile 23
Betchworth: $\frac{1}{4}$ mile at mile 26
Reigate: 1 mile at mile 30

Merstham: 200 yards at mile 33
Oxted: 1 mile at mile 31
Dunton Green: $\frac{1}{2}$ mile at mile 52
Otford: on Path at mile 55
Cuxton: $\frac{1}{2}$ mile at mile 70
Rochester: 2 miles at mile 71
Hollingbourne: $\frac{3}{4}$ mile at mile 86
Harrietsham: $\frac{1}{2}$ mile at mile 88
Lenham: 1 mile at mile 89
Charing: $\frac{1}{2}$ mile at mile 94
Wye: on Path at mile 100
Folkestone: $1\frac{1}{2}$ miles at mile 116
Dover: on Path

Railway Stations on the Canterbury loop
Chilham: $\frac{1}{2}$ mile at mile C5
Chartham: 1 mile at mile C9
Canterbury: on Path at mile C13
Bekesbourne: $\frac{1}{2}$ mile at mile C16
Snowdown: 1 mile at mile C21
Shepherdswell (Sibertswold): $\frac{1}{4}$ mile at mile C24

Accommodation

The North Downs Way has much accommodation near it. In addition to the traditional bed-and-breakfast accommodation found in private houses, there are a considerable number of hotels and inns in the larger towns along the route, which provide accommodation but which are likely to be considerably more expensive. There is an accommodation list arranged geographically from west to east on pp. 147–8. (The author would be grateful for any suitable additions on this list for inclusion in future editions of the guide. Please write to him c/o Penguin Books Ltd, 536 Kings Road, London SW10 OUH.)

There are not many Youth Hostels along the route. Those there are lie some considerable distance from the Path. The most convenient are Ewhurst Green, 6 miles off the route near mile 18; Holmbury St Mary, 2 miles off the route at mile 19; Tanners Hatch, 1 mile off the route at mile 21; Crockham Hill, 6 miles off the route at mile 45; Kemsing, $\frac{1}{4}$ mile off the route at mile 55; Doddington, $3\frac{1}{2}$ miles off the route at mile 91; and there are hostels at Canterbury, mile 14, and Dover.

Facilities for backpackers are very limited, but what is available is listed at the end of the guide. Never camp without first seeking the landowner's permission. Even though some of the woods along the route may seem to make inviting overnight stops, you will be turned off unceremoniously if you are discovered by a farmer or gamekeeper.

Clothing and equipment

No special clothing or equipment is required to walk this lowland path. Stout footwear and a waterproof anorak and over-trousers are all that is required. Obviously, if the purse allows it it is better to buy a cagoule, anorak or waterproof walking jacket. Avoid wearing jeans as they usually cut far too tight for comfort and are miserably cold when wet. Breeches or an old pair of light worsted trousers tucked into long woollen socks are much more satisfactory. In summer, shorts may be worn, but do beware of sunburn.

All walkers will require a suitable rucksack. Day walkers will have to carry food and drink and foul-weather gear. Never on any account rely solely on public houses and cafés for food and drink, as they may be sold out when you arrive or you may be delayed and arrive to find them closed. Those backpacking, bed-and-breakfasting or Youth-Hostelling will require a rucksack large enough to contain all that they need. The weight of all equipment, kit and food carried in the rucksack should not exceed 30lb. Backpackers can keep down the weight by sharing certain items of gear such as tents, cooking equipment and food. Unless it is possible to persuade a relative or friend to deliver and collect you from the termini of the path, most wayfarers walking the route on consecutive days will find it more convenient to use public transport.

How to use the guide

The purpose of this guide is to provide all the information that the walker requires to enable him to walk the route of the North Downs Way either from the east or from the west. The main body of the guide comprises strip maps of the route on a scale of 1:25000 (approx 2½ ins. to 1 mile) which show the route in very great detail, with such information as the location of gates, stiles, signposts and waymarks which the Ordnance Survey do not show on their maps. In addition, although based on the Ordnance Survey maps (with the sanction of the Controller of Her Majesty's Stationery Office), they have been updated by means of personal survey and are thus more accurate.

A great deal of thought has gone into the design of the maps and they must be studied carefully in conjunction with the key in order to get the most from them. In order to reduce the amount of unnecessary detail and to avoid cluttering them unduly, contour and grid lines have been omitted. Instead, grid line numbers form the frame of each map so that it is possible to relate them to any Ordnance Survey map and to use a compass if required. Instead of indicating heights in the conventional way a profile of the path is shown in half scale at the bottom of every map. The numbers on the path profile relate to the mile numbers shown on the map. In this way it is possible to see at a glance whether the section of the route to be walked is easy or strenuous.

North, although always indicated, is of academic interest only and is not usually at the top of the page as the guide is designed to be held in the natural reading position. Those travelling eastwards towards Dover start at the front of the guide and those travelling westwards towards Farnham start at the back of the guide.

Opposite every map is the relevant section of text. There are instructions on how to follow the route in either direction and there are brief notes of interesting things to be seen along the way. Useful information given in the text includes the location of shops, banks, post offices, cafés, restaurants and public houses. Early closing days are given, together with brief details of the availability of public transport.

Great care has been taken in the compilation of this guide but walkers should be aware that the countryside is constantly changing and that time may render parts of it out of date. The author would be most grateful for comments and criticism as well as information about any changes which may have occurred. (Please write to him c/o Penguin Books Ltd, 536 Kings Road, London SW10 0UH.) Neither the author nor the publisher can accept any responsibility for the consequences incurred if the walker departs from the right of way.

The guide is intended to be complete in itself and to contain everything that the walker needs to know. However, some walkers like to have a general map which will place the route in the general context of the surrounding countryside. If the map on p. 26 does not contain sufficient detail, the reader is recommended to buy sheets 9 and 10 of Bartholomews National Map Series on a scale of 1:100000. These excellent maps mark the North Downs Way and it is easy to relate the route to the roads and rail system in the surrounding countryside.

The Pilgrims' Way

The North Downs Way and the Pilgrims' Way are identified in the popular mind with a route running from Winchester to Canterbury which was supposed to be used by pilgrims on their way to the shrine of St Thomas à Becket. The writer who first made the theory popular was Hilaire Belloc (1870–1953), who wrote, in 1904, an agreeable and entertaining book called *The Old Road* which professed to re-discover the route that the pilgrims were supposed to have taken. Belloc was a man of strong opinions who was wont to express them forcibly, with wit and considerable literary style. But although he had occasional flashes of historical insight, modern historians regard most of his views as eccentric.

Let us now examine the possibility that pilgrims *did* use this route. Winchester was the capital of England in Saxon times. William the Conqueror was crowned in both London and Winchester and it was not until the twelfth century that London became the undisputed capital of England. Winchester had its own saint in Swithun, now remembered mainly as a weather forecaster but then the centre of a considerable cult. It was a prosperous city and had trade links with the Continent through the export of wool from Southampton, and there is evidence that many pilgrims, including some from mainland Europe, came to worship at the shrine of St Swithun.

After the murder of Thomas à Becket in 1170, the cult of St Swithun declined in popularity, but many pilgrims still took the opportunity of praying at both shrines and there was a steady stream of traffic between Winchester and Canterbury. Some probably took the direct route via Guildford, Dorking, Reigate, Westerham, Sevenoaks and Maidstone, but even by medieval standards the roads were bad (until the improvement of the A25 and the construction of the M25 it was a slow and frustrating journey by car) and C. G. Crump in an article in Volume XXI of *History* has argued convincingly that most would have gone via London to Canterbury: 'In the fourteenth century they went from Winchester to Alresford, not by the lanes up the Itchen ... but by the straight road over the downs, and so by Alton and

Farnham to Guildford. From Guildford they went up to London by Ripley and Kingston, as men go today; and from London they went, like Chaucer's pilgrims, to Canterbury. And that road is marked on the fourteenth-century map in the Bodleian Library, of which Richard Gough published a facsimile in the first volume of his *British Topography* in 1780.'

The earliest mention of the name Pilgrims' Way occurs in the eighteenth century, so the name was given to it long after the pilgrimages had ceased. What has come to be known as the Pilgrims' Way is actually a prehistoric trackway. The chalk hills of southern England made natural routes for prehistoric man because they are dry, the vegetation was sparser than in the clay valleys below and the narrow ridges of chalk form natural well-defined routes which were used for trading and, possibly, for pilgrimages to important cultural and religious centres such as Stonehenge and Avebury. The modern long-distance footpath follows this ancient trackway for considerable stretches, but much of it has been incorporated into the modern road network, as for example over the Hog's Back between Farnham and Guildford.

Pilgrims and Pilgrimages

Pilgrimages formed an important part of the social life of the Middle Ages and it is helpful to have some idea of their importance and purpose. According to Catholic theology, those who die in mortal sin are condemned to everlasting punishment in hell. Forgiveness is available to those who truly repent of their sins and seek forgiveness, but God still requires punishment to make the soul perfect in His sight. Punishment takes place in purgatory, where the souls of those who are ultimately to go to heaven are confined. There exists, however, a vast treasury of merits built up by the sufferings of Christ and the virtues of the Blessed Virgin and the Saints, and the Church, by her power of jurisdiction, has the right of administering the benefit of these merits in consideration of prayers or other pious works. In other words, the Church has the power to commute the time spent in purgatory. During the Middle Ages one of the most popular ways of obtaining an indulgence (remission of time in purgatory) was to go on a pilgrimage or to fight in the crusades. These pilgrimages were not necessarily solemn affairs but were often occasions of great joy, feasting and general jollity, rather like an outing to Blackpool. Indulgences were the subject of much corruption and abuse. Charlatans, known as pardoners, sold them, and others obtained indulgences for third parties by being paid for going on a pilgrimage in somebody else's stead.

A place that was a centre of pilgrimage brought great wealth both to the ecclesiastical authorities and to the local townsfolk, and many churches had relics which were venerated by the faithful. Some of these were clearly spurious, such as phials containing the breath of Christ or Our Lady's milk, the tip of Lucifer's tail, the tooth of St John and the sound of the bells of Solomon's Temple kept in a bottle.

St Thomas à Becket

Canterbury was the most important see in England; it was founded by St Augustine and was the place from which the Roman form of Christianity was introduced into England. It had always been a centre of pilgrimage, but after the murder of Thomas à Becket it achieved an entirely new significance, and together with Jerusalem, Rome and Compostela became one of the most important centres of pilgrimage in Christendom.

In our secular age it is easy to overlook the importance of the struggle between Becket and the Church and Henry II; but the quarrel was serious and the outcome important. Becket had taken minor orders and was appointed Archdeacon of Canterbury in 1154. He was a most able man. In 1155 Henry II made him his Chancellor and he became an intimate friend and adviser to the King. During this period he could not be described as a saintly man and took part in all the pleasures to which his rank entitled him. Under the feudal system the King, provided he could keep the loyalty of his barons, was, in effect, a despot and the only other significant power in the land belonged to the Church. The influence wielded by the Church was not just that of a moral voice, but was based upon real power. The Church, after the King, was the biggest landowner in the country and controlled vast estates. Moreover, in an age where Christianity was not questioned and most people had a very lively sense of the reality of hell-fire, the ecclesiastical authorities had a powerful weapon which they did not hesitate to use.

Henry believed that if Thomas was appointed Archbishop of Canterbury their long friendship would make him a great ally and he would be in an unrivalled position as a powerful King with the Church on his side. Thomas was reluctant to accept, because he knew it would be the end of his friendship with Henry and, as events turned out, this proved to be true. From his election to the see in 1162, Thomas changed his life-style, resigned the Chancellorship of England and soon found himself in dispute with the King. The King wished to regulate relations between Church and state and put forward a set of articles known as the Constitutions of Clarendon. Thomas refused to sign these because one article was offensive to the Church in that it attempted to make those in clerical orders subject to the secular courts rather than to the religious courts as previously. In the Middle Ages a cleric was anyone who took minor orders (an office in the church below that of Deacon), so this included a significant proportion of the population, for the minor orders comprised porters, lectors (liturgical readers), exorcists and acolytes (those assisting at mass). The quarrel grew worse and at one stage the Pope threatened an interdict which would have had the effect of banning the whole population of England from the Sacraments, an appalling punishment at the time. Eventually a reconciliation took place, but Becket again annoyed the King who, in an unguarded moment of exasperation, uttered the fateful words 'Who will rid me of this turbulent Priest?' Four knights set off for Canterbury, found Becket in his cathedral and murdered him before the altar. There is not much doubt that Henry was too astute a politician to have connived in the murder of Becket, but the deed was done, there was much ill feeling against the King and, with almost indecent haste, Thomas was canonized scarcely two years after his death. Henry was forced to do public penance by walking barefoot through Canterbury and being flogged before Becket's shrine. Before long pilgrims were flocking to Canterbury to gain the indulgences which were attached to their journey, the Norman cathedral was transformed into a magnificent Gothic structure and the Church waxed fat on the profits. During the later Middle Ages, the popularity of pilgrimages declined but they did not cease until the Reformation and the Dissolution of the monasteries, when Henry VIII took particular care to destroy the shrine of St Thomas at Canterbury.

Book List

Footpath Guides

Allen, David J., and Imrie, Patrick R., *Discovering the North Downs Way,* Shire Publications, 1980.

Doggett, Tom, and Trevelyan, John, *The North Downs Way,* Ramblers' Association, 1979.

Herbstein, Denis, *The North Downs Way,* HMSO, 1982.

North Downs Way Maps, published by the Countryside Commission, 1978.

Wright, C. J., *A Guide to the Pilgrims' Way and the North Downs Way,* 2nd edn, Constable, 1977.

Geology

Gallois, R. W., *The Wealden Basin,* British Regional Geology, HMSO, 1965.

Sherlock, R. L., *London and the Thames Basin,* British Regional Geology, HMSO, 1960.

The Pilgrims' Way

Belloc, Hilaire, *The Old Road,* 2nd edn, Constable, 1910.

Cartwright, Julia, *The Pilgrims' Way,* Murray, 1911.

Crump, C. G., 'The Pilgrims' Way', in *History,* vol. XXI.

Jennett, Sean, *The Pilgrims' Way,* Constable, 1971.

Pilgrims and Pilgrimages

Erasmus, Desiderius, *Pilgrimage to St Mary of Walsingham and St Thomas of Canterbury* (1540), ed. J. G. Nichols, Murray, 1875.

Finucane, Ronald C., *Miracles and Pilgrims: Popular Beliefs in Medieval England,* Dent, 1977.

Hall, Donald, *English Medieval Pilgrimages,* Routledge, 1966.

Heath, Sidney, *Pilgrim Life in the Middle Ages,* Fisher Unwin, 1911.

Jusserand, J. J., *English Wayfaring Life in the Middle Ages,* Fisher Unwin, 1920.

Loxton, Howard, *Pilgrimage to Canterbury,* David & Charles, 1978.

Snowden-Ward, H., *The Canterbury Pilgrimages,* 2nd edn, Black, 1927.

Sumption, Jonathan, *Pilgrimage: An Image of Medieval Religion,* Faber, 1975.

Watt, Francis, *Canterbury Pilgrims and Their Ways,* Methuen, 1917.

Thomas à Becket

Duggan, Alfred, *Thomas à Becket of Canterbury,* Faber, 1967.

Knowles, David, *Thomas Becket,* Black, 1970.

Williamson, Hugh Ross, *The Arrow and the Sword,* Faber, 1947.

Winston, Richard, *Thomas Becket,* Constable, 1967.

Kent

Bignell, Alan, *Kent Villages,* Hale, 1975.

Boorman, H. R. Pratt, *Kent, Our County,* Kent Messenger, 1979.

Boyle, John, *Portrait of Canterbury,* 2nd edn, Hale, 1980.

Boyle, John, *Rural Kent,* Hale, 1976.

Burnham, C. P., and McCrae, Stuart, *Kent: The Garden of England,* Paul Norbury Publications, 1978.

Clarke, Dennis, *Otford in Kent: A History,* Otford and District Historical Society, 1975.

Complete Tourist's Guide and Handbook to the Ancient City of Rochester, John Hallewell Publications, 1979.

Glover, Judith, *The Batsford Colour Book of Kent,* Batsford, 1976.

Green, Ivan, *The Book of Dover,* Barracuda Books, 1978.

Green, Ivan, *Yesterday's Town, Dover,* Barracuda Books, 1980.

Higham, Roger, *Kent,* Batsford, 1974.

Hill, Derek Ingram, *Christ's Glorious Church: The Story of Canterbury Cathedral,* SPCK, 1976.

Hillier, Caroline, *The Bulwark Shore,* Eyre Methuen, 1980 (an account of the Kent coastline).

Jessup, Frank W., *A History of Kent,* 2nd edn, Phillimore, 1974.

Kent, Joan, *Binder Twine and Rabbit Stew,* Bailey & Swinfen, 1976.

Kent, Joan, *Wood Smoke and Pigeon Pie,* Bailey & Swinfen, 1977.

Lang-Sims, Lois, *Canterbury Cathedral: Mother Church of the Holy Trinity,* Cassell, 1979.

Malcolm, John, *Around Historic Kent,* Midas Books, 1978.

Newman, John, *The Buildings of England: North-East and East Kent,* Penguin Books, 1969.

Newman, John, *The Buildings of England: West Kent and the Weald,* Penguin Books, 1969.

Oliver, John, *Dickens' Rochester,* John Hallewell Publications, 1978.

Rootes, Andrew, *Front Line County,* Hale 1980 (the wartime bombing of Kent).

Smith, F. F., *A History of Rochester* (1928), John Hallewell Publications, 1976.

Turpin, B. J., and Turpin, J. M., *Windmills in Kent: A Guide to Existing Windmills in the County,* Windmill Publications, 1979.

Underhill, Francis, *The Story of Rochester Cathedral,* British Publishing Co., 1969.

Victoria County History of Kent.

Webb, William, *Kent's Historic Buildings,* Black, 1977.

West, Jenny, *The Windmills of Kent,* Skelton, 1973.

Wright, Christopher, *Kent Through the Years,* Batsford, 1975.

Surrey

Baker, John L., *A Picture of Surrey,* Hale, 1980.

Brandon, Peter, *A History of Surrey,* Phillimore, 1977.

Chapman, G., and Young, R., *Box Hill,* Serendip Fine Books, 1979.

Cracknell, Basil E., *Portrait of Surrey,* 2nd edn, Hale, 1974.

Fraser, Maxwell, *Surrey,* Batsford, 1975.

Hooper, Wilfrid, *Reigate: Its Story Through the Ages* (1948), Kohler & Coombes, 1979.

Jekyll, Gertrude, *Old West Surrey: Some Notes and Memories* (1904), Kohler & Coombes, 1978.

Knight, David and others, *Dorking, Past and Present,* Kohler & Coombes, 1980.

Kohler, Margaret K., *Memories of Old Dorking,* Kohler & Coombes, 1977.

Malden, Henry Elliot, *A History of Surrey* (1908), EP Publishing, 1977.

Nairn, Ian, and Pevsner, Nikolaus, *The Buildings of England: Surrey,* Penguin Books, 1962.

Salmon, John E., editor, *The Surrey Countryside: The Interplay of the Land and the People,* University of Surrey, 1975.
Victoria County History of Surrey.
Watkin, Bruce, *Surrey,* Faber, 1977.

General

Jefferies, Richard, *Nature near London* (1893), John Clare Books, 1980.
White, John Talbot, *The South-East, Down and Weald: Kent, Surrey and Sussex,* Eyre Methuen, 1977.

Guide and Sectional Maps

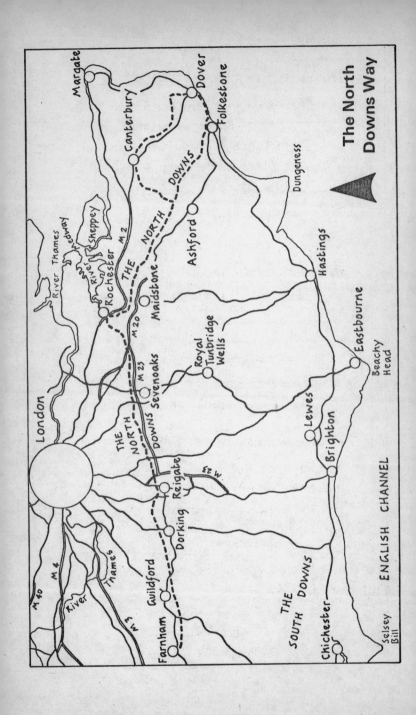

The North Downs Way

KEY

• • • • • • • • • • • The North Downs Way

———————— Route on metalled surface

(73) Distance in miles from Farnham

• • • • • • Other visible paths or tracks

┄┄┄┄┄ Hedge   ┄┄┄┄┄ Fence

Woodland   ☀ Tumulus

Quarry   ▲ Triangulation column

▪▪▪ Buildings (only shown to aid navigation)

+ Church   ▲ Youth Hostel

════════ Major road

———————— Minor road

════════ Other road

▨▨▨▨▨▨ Motorway

▪━▪━▪━━●━ Railway with
station

F : Footpath sign

B : Bridleway sign   ◀ Direction of North

N : North Downs Way sign   River with direction of flow

W : Waymark   FB Footbridge

S : Stile   The numbers in the margin

G : Gate   locate the Northings and
Eastings (Grid Lines) on

D : Double Gate   Ordnance Survey maps

55

03

Gradient profile of route showing
milepoints and height in feet

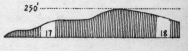

250'
17   18

1. Farnham, Compton, Thumblands

2 miles
Maps: 1:25000 sheet SU84; 1:50000 sheet 186

East-bound: The North Downs Way starts at the traffic lights on the A31, the Farnham by-pass, between the town centre and the railway station. Walk towards Guildford, keeping to the right-hand side of the road, and after 200 yds turn right down an un-metalled lane. At the river, bear left at a gate between the house and the river, pass under a railway bridge and cross a stile to reach a road. Turn left, follow the road and take the first turning on the left, signposted Moor Park College. At the crossroads, continue forward and at the top of the hill, where the road bears round to the right, leave the road to continue forward to cross a stile. Cross another stile to the other side of the fence and go forward, still following the fence. Continue in this direction for ¼ mile, crossing several stiles and walking through woods, until reaching a sunken track. Turn right and shortly left past a modern bungalow and into an expensive housing development to reach a road.

West-bound: Turn down beside No. 44, follow the estate road and walk parallel to the driveway of a modern bungalow on the left. On reaching a sunken track, turn right and 200 yds later turn left over a stile. Walk through woods and fields to a road and then continue forward downhill, over some crossroads to a T-junction. Turn right, follow the road for 200 yds

and bear right over a stile. On reaching another stile, turn left and follow a track which turns sharp right after 100 yds and then passes under the railway. Bear left and follow the river bank. This well-defined path will bring you to the A31. Continue forward to the traffic lights where you should turn left for the railway station or right for the town centre.

Farnham (population 33,000) has a Tourist Information Centre in South Street (tel. Godalming 4104), buses to Guildford, Alton, Alresford, Winchester, South-ampton, Godalming, Seale, Sands, Haslemere and Aldershot. Early closing day is Wednesday. (*For a description of Farnham see p. 142.*)

Moor Park College was built in 1630 for Sir William Temple. His secretary was Jonathan Swift, who wrote *Tale of a Tub* while living in the house. He also acted as tutor to Esther Johnson, whom he immortalized as Stella.

A mile down the valley is a cave known as St Mary's Well in which once lived Mother Ludlam, a notorious witch. Nearby are the sad ruins of Waverley Abbey, the first Cistercian house in England, founded in about 1128 by William Giffard, Bishop of Winchester. This once noble abbey fell into ruin after the Dissolution of the Monasteries and now gives its name to the District Council formed after the reorganization of local government in 1974.

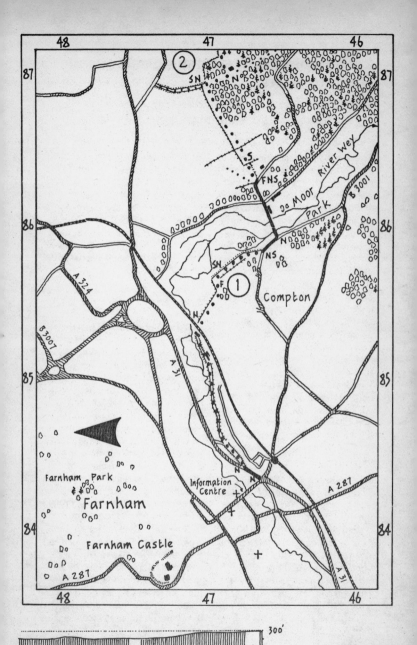

2. Thumblands, The Sands, Seale, Hampton Park

3 miles
Maps: 1:25000 sheets S U84 and S U94; 1:50000 sheet 186

East-bound: On reaching the road turn left for a few yards and then right through an enclosed path. In a short time you will reach a road, at which point turn right, and then left at the club house. Near Binton Cottage, where the road bears left, take the path which goes off to the right cross the road and continue along the track on the other side. After about 300 yds leave the obvious track, cross the stile to the right, walk to another stile and continue forward, keeping a hedge on your left. This will bring you to another road. Turn right at this point and, a few yards later, turn left off the road through a wood. On reaching a barrier at the edge of the wood, turn left for 100 yds or so to a stile, then turn right and follow the edge of the wood across fields and past another wood to reach the road (see next map).

West-bound: Follow the path along the edge of fields and woods until coming to a stile on the left. Cross this stile, walk down the edge of the wood for 100 yds or so and then turn right and you will soon come to the road. Turn right at the road and very shortly left, keeping a hedge on your right. This will bring you to a sandy track and a stile. Continue forward following the enclosed track to a road, cross it and pass along the edge of the golf course until reaching the road. Turn left at the road and at the T-junction turn right. After $\frac{1}{4}$ mile, you will see on your left, just before reaching the road junction, an enclosed path. Walk down this to the next road, turn left for a few yards and then turn right beside No. 44 into a small development.

The Sands, just off the Path, has a post office stores and a public house.

Seale, just off the Path, nestles underneath the Hog's Back. The parish church of St Lawrence is built of clunch, a very hard chalk, and dates from the twelfth century, although much of what can be seen now is fifteenth-century work. It may have been founded by nearby Waverley Abbey. It contains a Norman font, some brasses and a monument to Ensign Long which shows in bas relief the collision of warships in which he died in 1809. Some authorities attribute the memorial verse to his friend Lord Byron.

The Hog's Back, clearly visible along much of this section, carries the main A31 road along a significant chalk ridge. There has been a road along this ridge since neolithic times and it may be that the name is derived from *ogof* (giant), a name often associated with ancient routes.

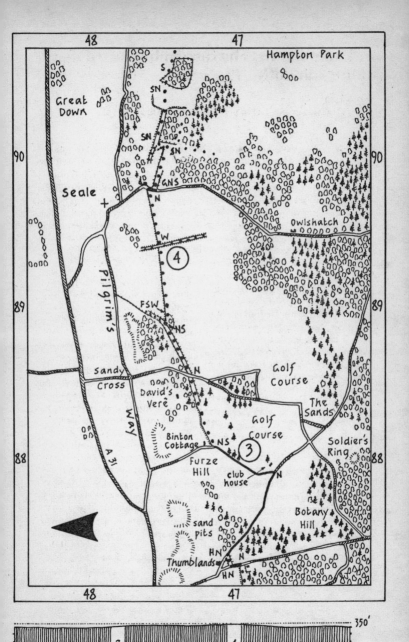

3. Totford Hatch, Lascombe, Puttenham, Puttenham Golf Course

2 miles
Maps: 1:25000 sheet SU94; 1:50000 sheet 186

East-bound: On reaching the road, which is the private drive to Hampton Park, turn left for a few yards and then right across a bridge over a stream. At point B, fork left at a faint waymark on a post, and continue along a grassy path to the metalled Lascombe Lane, just past the farm in a dip. Walk through Puttenham past the church to meet the main road. Turn right (signposted Godalming) and, opposite the Jolly Farmer public house, turn left and follow the metalled lane which runs past the car park. Where the lane turns sharp left continue forward along the track which runs beside the golf course.

West-bound: Follow the clear path beside the golf course until reaching a metalled lane. Continue forward to the main road opposite the Jolly Farmer public house, turn right and very shortly left into the village of Puttenham. Follow the road right through the village and continue up Lascombe Lane. About 200 yds later fork right and continue until the metalling ceases. Walk down the side of a farm in a dell and at point C be sure to fork right and follow the edge of the wood. At point A west-bound walkers leave the sandy track and continue forward to cross the stream and reach the estate road. Turn left for a few yards along the road to a gate and then turn right and follow the path through the wood.

Puttenham has a grocer's shop, May's Place, on the western outskirts, which closes on Thursday afternoons but is open on Sunday mornings. There is a public house, the Good Intent, with a punning sign depicting Cromwell praying in his tent. It serves good bar snacks. The post office stores closes half day on Wednesday.

Puttenham parish church was built in the first half of the twelfth century and contains some good Norman work, although the tower dates from the fifteenth century. Originally it had a spire, but this was burnt as a result of a fire at the nearby blacksmiths. In 1972 the village well inside the churchyard was discovered under remarkable circumstances when a cypress tree suddenly dropped down it. Puttenham Priory, a beautiful Palladian house behind the church, was built in 1762.

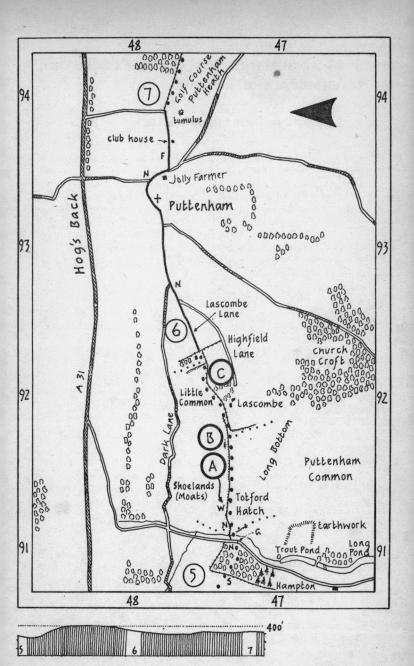

48　　　　　　47

94　　　　　　94

Golf Course
Puttenham Heath

⑦

＊ tumulus

club house →

F

N　　■ Jolly Farmer

✝ Puttenham

Hog's Back

93　　　　　　93

A 31

N

Lascombe
Lane

⑥

Highfield
Lane

Church
Croft

C

Little
Common

Lascombe

92　　　　　　92

Dark Lane

B

A

Long Bottom

Puttenham
Common

Shoelands
(Moats)

W

Totford
Hatch

N

G

Earthwork

91　　　　　　91

N

Trout Pond

Long
Pond

⑤

S

Hampton

48　　　　　　47

400'

5　　　　　6　　　　　7

33

4. Monkgrove Copse, The Watts Gallery, Loseley Park

2½ miles
Maps: 1:25000 sheet SU94; 1:50000 sheet 186

East-bound: Follow the edge of the golf course and then cross Compton Heath, ignoring paths which cross. Pass under the A3 and continue to a road. Turn left and almost immediately turn right along a track off the road past the Watts Gallery, which will bring you to a road (see Map 5).

West-bound: Follow the clear track alongside Loseley Park past the Watts Gallery to a road. Turn left at the road and then almost immediately right, pass under the A3, and then fork left along a clear track. Ignore paths which cross and you will arrive at the golf course.

Compton has a post office stores, early closing Wednesday and Saturday, a public house, the Harrow, and buses to Guildford, Farnham, Godalming and Cranleigh. The parish church of St Nicholas is well worth visiting as it has a Saxon tower and other Saxon work incorporated in the later Norman rebuilding. But what makes it particularly remarkable is the way the sanctuary has been converted into two storeys connected by a wooden staircase. The sanctuary arch is protected by a balustrade which is believed to date from about the end of the twelfth century and is probably the oldest piece of ecclesiastical woodwork in the country. Nobody is quite certain why the sanctuary has two storeys, but it has been suggested that a relic was kept in the upper storey. The church also contains an anchorite's cell and it is believed that the six skeletons discovered close to the church in 1906 may have been those of the hermits who occupied these cells. In the cemetery is a terracotta chapel designed by Mary Fraser-Tyler, the wife of the painter George Frederick Watts. The interior is covered with huge angel figures and medallions. Watts and his wife lived at Limnerslease in the village, and beside the North Downs Way is the art gallery that Mrs Watts built to house her husband's works which is open to the public and is well worth visiting.

Loseley House was built in the middle of the sixteenth century by Sir William Moore, who plundered Waverley Abbey for stones for his new house.

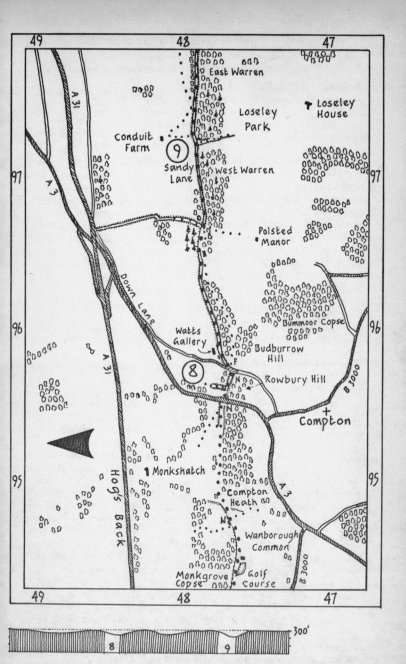

5. Piccard's Farm, Guildford, South Warren Farm

2½ miles
Maps: 1:25000 sheets SU94 and TQ04; 1:50000 sheet 186

East-bound: On reaching the road at a hairpin bend, turn left and take the farm track which, after 100 yds or so, turns right and runs through Piccard's Farm to rejoin the road near the A3100. Turn right opposite the Ship Inn and almost immediately left down the metalled Ferry Lane, which will bring you to the banks of the Wey. Turn left and follow the Path along the river bank to the footbridge. Cross the bridge to reach the A281, turn right and walk for ¼ mile or so until turning left along the metalled Pilgrims' Way. Where it bears to the left, fork right and follow a rough track past a car park to reach Chantry Cottage. Take the track on the left of the cottage signposted St Martha's.

West-bound: Follow the clear track to Chantry Cottage then bear right past the car park to meet the metalled Pilgrims' Way. Turn left and follow it to the A281. Turn right and walk along the main road for ¼ mile or so, looking for a prominent footbridge on the left, where the river almost touches the road. Cross the footbridge, turn left and follow the bank of the Wey to the old ferry landing stage. Turn right and climb up the bank into Ferry Lane to reach the A3100. Turn right and then almost immediately left, opposite the Ship, and after 200 yds turn right off the road to follow the track to Piccard's Farm. Beyond Piccard's Farm the track turns sharp left to reach a road with a hairpin bend. Turn right at this point and take the clear track.

Guildford (population of 60,000) is an important shopping centre and market town. There are bus services to Winchester, Southampton, Farnham, London, Chalford, Chilworth, Newlands Corner, Shere, Gomshall and Dorking, and rail services to London, Farnham, Portsmouth, Basingstoke, Southampton and the west of England, Shalford, Chilworth, Gomshall, Dorking, Redhill, Edenbridge and Tonbridge. Early closing day and market day is Wednesday. There is a tourist information centre at Civic Hall, London Road (tel. Guildford 67314). (*For a description of Guildford see p. 142.*)

St Catherine's chapel, on the little hill just off the path near the River Wey, was built in the fourteenth century and is now a ruin. In Ferry Lane is a fanciful notice alleging that Chaucer's pilgrims came this way. The pilgrims *did* come this way, but not the band described by Chaucer, for they took the direct route from Southwark to Canterbury.

Shalford has a post office, a grocer's shop, a bus service to Horsham, Plaistow, Guildford, Cranleigh, Ewhurst, Shere, Gomshall and Dorking and train services to Guildford, Reigate, Redhill, Edenbridge, Tonbridge, Chilworth, Shere, Gomshall, Reading and London.

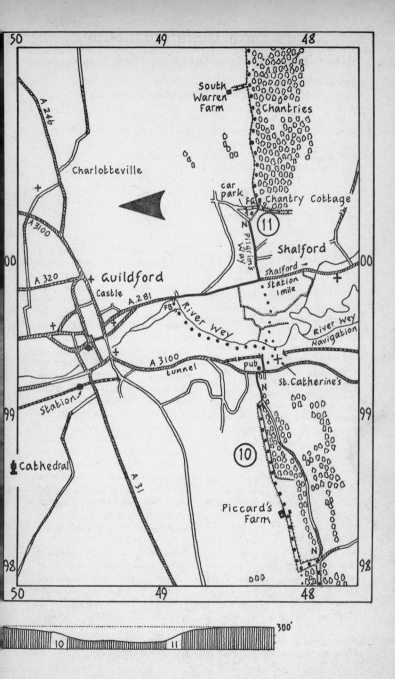

South
Warren
Farm

Chantries

A 246

Charlotteville

car
park

FB

Chantry Cottage

⑪

N

Pilgrim's
Way

Shalford

A 3100

Shalford
Station
1 mile

Guildford

A 320

Castle

A 281

FB

River Wey

River Wey
Navigation

A 3100
tunnel

pub

St. Catherine's

N

Station

⑩

Cathedral

A 31

Piccard's
Farm

N

300'

10

11

6. Whinny Hill, St Martha's Hill, Newlands Corner

3 miles
Maps: 1:25000 sheet TQ04; 1:50000 sheet 186

East-bound: The Path follows a clear track from Whinny Hill to the road, turns left along the road for a few yards and then right along the track that leads to St Martha's. At the foot of St Martha's Hill keep to the very wide path which runs forward through the pines. Beyond St Martha's be sure to fork left along a minor track just before reaching a pill box. At the road, turn left and take the narrow path which has been constructed along the left-hand side of the road. Where this rejoins the road turn right and follow the path along the edge of the wood to Newlands Corner. It is easy to get lost in the huge car park at Newlands Corner, so it is probably better to take the car park exit to the main A25 road. Turn right along the road for a short distance and look for the North Downs Way sign which points along the wide track on the left of the road.

West-bound: On reaching the A25 at Newlands Corner, turn right and make for the entrance to the car park. At the end of the car park follow the broad grassy path, which tends to drop downhill following the edge of the wood, until reaching a road. Cross the road and turn left downhill to follow a path which has been constructed beside the road. On reaching a house where the road bears round to the left, turn right along the signposted path which will bring you to a very broad track where you should turn right and walk to the top of St Martha's Hill. Continue down to the road, turn left for a few yards and then right down another track.

Chilworth, 1 mile off the Path, has a grocer's shop (closed half-day Thursday, open Sunday morning), a post office (closed Wednesday and Saturday afternoon) and a public house. There are bus services to Guildford, Shalford, Shere, Gomshall, Westcott and Dorking and train services to Guildford, Gomshall, Dorking, Redhill, Tonbridge and Reading. The chapel of St Martha is actually the parish church of Chilworth, 500 ft below in the valley. The dedication to St Martha is possibly a corruption of St Martyrs, for there is a tradition that 600 Christians suffered martyrdom about the year AD 600 and it may be that this established a local shrine. Originally Norman, the church was almost completely rebuilt in the nineteenth century. In the churchyard is a headstone commemorating the actress Yvonne Arnaud, whose ashes were scattered on the hill.

Newlands Corner has a gigantic car park, toilets, a snack bar and a bus service to Guildford, Shere, Gomshall, Ewhurst and Cranleigh. It has splendid views over the Tillingbourne valley but, alas, it has been sadly desecrated.

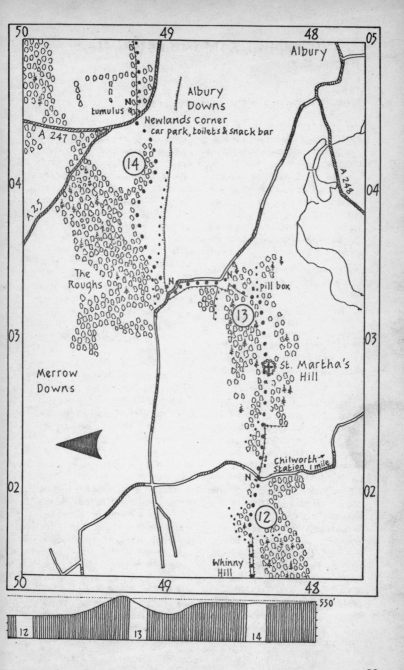

Albury

Albury
Downs

tumulus

Newlands Corner
car park, toilets & snack bar

A 247

14

A 25

A 248

The
Roughs

pill box

13

Merrow
Downs

St. Martha's
Hill

Chilworth
Station 1 mile

12

Whinny
Hill

550'

12   13   14

7. Netherlands, Hollister Farm, Great Kings Wood

$2\frac{1}{4}$ miles
Maps: 1:25000 sheet TQ04; 1:50000 sheet 187

East-bound: Follow the clear track through the trees and on reaching the road near mile 16 continue forward until reaching another road. Turn right here for a few yards and then left down a metalled lane leading to Hollister Farm. At Hollister Farm turn sharp left and follow the metalled lane through the woods.

West-bound: Follow the metalled lane to Hollister Farm to where it turns sharp right and then joins the road in about 300 yds. Turn right here along the road and in a few yards turn left along a track, which crosses a road and then continues through the woods to reach the A25 at Newlands Corner.

This is a dull section lacking in views because the route lies through thick woods. Albury, $\frac{3}{4}$ mile off the Path, has a post office stores (open Sunday mornings, closed half-day Saturday) and a public house. Near the entrance to Albury Park is a Victorian Gothic church erected in 1840 by the Catholic Apostolic Church, which looked upon the Pope as a heretic. The gardens of Albury House were laid out by the diarist John Evelyn, who lived a little further down the valley at Wotton during the last quarter of the seventeenth century. In the grounds are the remains of a Saxon church comprising a nave and chancel which was somewhat altered by the Normans. In the mid eighteenth century the spire was removed, a cupola was added and the south chapel converted into a private mortuary for the Drummond family, who owned Albury House.

Shere, $\frac{3}{4}$ mile off the Path, is a most attractive village. It has a grocer's shop, a post office, two public houses, tea rooms and a restaurant. Early closing is Saturday and there are bus services to Dorking, Westcott, Gomshall, Chilworth, Guildford, Ewhurst and Cranleigh.

The parish church of St James contains a lot of Norman work and may stand on the site of an earlier Saxon church. It contains a Norman font of Purbeck marble and a crusader chest, used to collect money for the crusades. In the chancel north wall was once a cell for an anchoress. As was the custom, she was walled up and her only contact with the outside world was a squint. It appears she was not entirely a willing prisoner – she once escaped and had to be thrust back into her cell. Shere was once a centre of smuggling and some of the houses still have cellars in which the contraband was stored.

The Silent Pool, midway between Albury and Shere at the junction of the A25 and A248, comprises two deep ponds formed by a dam. The upper pond can be reached by a public path and is a popular beauty spot.

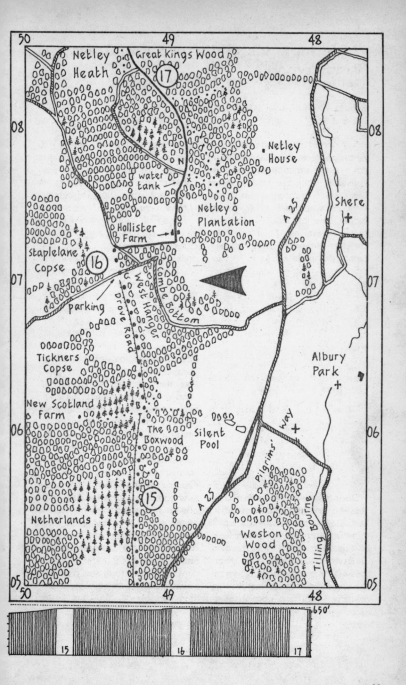

8. Great Kings Wood, Netley Heath, Hackhurst Downs, White Downs

3 miles
Maps: 1:25000 sheets TQ04 and TQ14; 1:50000 sheet 187

East-bound: About 300 yds after passing the junction of tracks at Gravelhill Gate, where the lane bears round to the right, look for a concrete water tank on the right hidden in some trees beside the path (nearby is the Hackhurst Downs National Trust sign). Leave the metalled lane at this point by turning right and then in a short distance fork left through the trees to reach some old war-time pill boxes and a road. Turn left at the road and a couple of hundred yards later look for a path which branches off to the right over White Downs.

West-bound: Follow the clear path from White Downs to the road. Turn left and look for a path that turns sharp right by a pill box. Follow this past another pill box, across Hackhurst Downs and then turn right to reach a metalled lane. Turn left along the lane and follow it all the way to Great Kings Wood.

During the war the whole of this area was used as a vast ammunition dump to store material for the invasion of France in 1944. It was at this time that the numerous concrete roads which criss-cross the area were constructed, as were the water tanks to be used in the event of fire. The pill boxes were built at the outbreak of war to provide a defensive line on the flank of the Downs against a possible German advance across southern England.

Gomshall, 1 mile off the Path, has a grocer's shop, a post office, a café, a restaurant, the Compasses public house, bus services to Dorking, Abinger Hammer, Shere, Guildford, Ewhurst and Cranleigh and trains to Reading, Guildford, Chilworth, Dorking, Redhill, Edenbridge and Tonbridge.

Abinger Hammer, 1 mile off the Path, has a post office stores (early closing Saturday), a café and the Abinger Arms public house, which serves snacks and has a restaurant. There are bus services to Dorking, Gomshall, Shere and Guildford. The hamlet gets its name to distinguish it from the village of Abinger and the Hammer refers to the numerous hammer ponds sited along the Tillingbourne which supplied power to work the forge hammers of the iron-making industry. The best-known sight in Abinger Hammer is the famous clock, dating from 1909, which overhangs the main road and has the hours struck by a figure wielding a hammer.

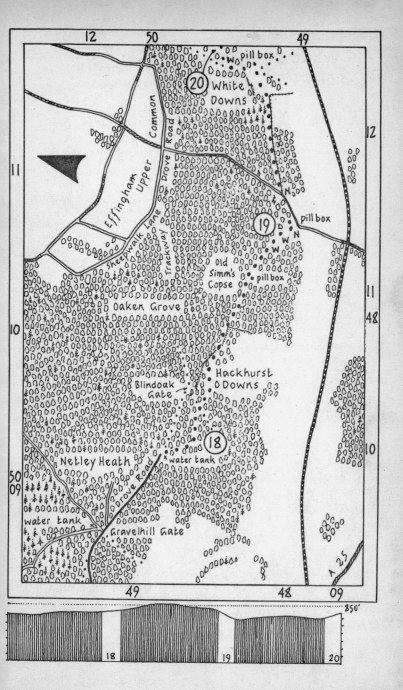

43

9. White Downs, Ranmore Common, Denbies

2¼ miles
Maps: 1:25000 sheets TQ14 and TQ15; 1:50000 sheet 187

East-bound: After mile 20 the Path follows the clearly defined route through the woods and crosses a major track near mile 21; ¼ mile later the track turns sharply to the left and at this point continue forward into a field and round the back of a house to meet the road at a stile. Walk down the road opposite, past Ranmore church, to where the road turns very sharply left. Turn right here along the driveway and then turn sharp left along another metalled carriageway.

West-bound: Follow the carriageway to a gate where it turns sharp right and joins the road on a bend, turn left and follow the road past Ranmore church. At the T-junction take the stile opposite, walk across a field and round the back of a house to reach an enclosed track. Continue forward along this track to mile 20.

Ranmore Common is owned by the National Trust and is a famous Surrey beauty spot where at weekends vast numbers of people congregate. The church was built in 1859 by Sir George Gilbert Scott for the Cubitts, the famous building family, who lived at nearby Denbies. It is a very fine example of Victorian church architecture as no expense was spared in its construction and decoration. It contains an elaborate font and frescoes by Reginald Frampton. In the churchyard is buried the founder of the church, Lord Ashcombe, whose father, Thomas Cubitt, began life in 1788 as a carpenter, set himself up in business and built extensively in London, including Belgrave Square and part of Buckingham Palace.

From Ranmore Common there are bus services to Guildford and Dorking.

Denbies was originally designed by Thomas Cubitt as a home for himself, but it has been demolished and the land belongs to the National Trust.

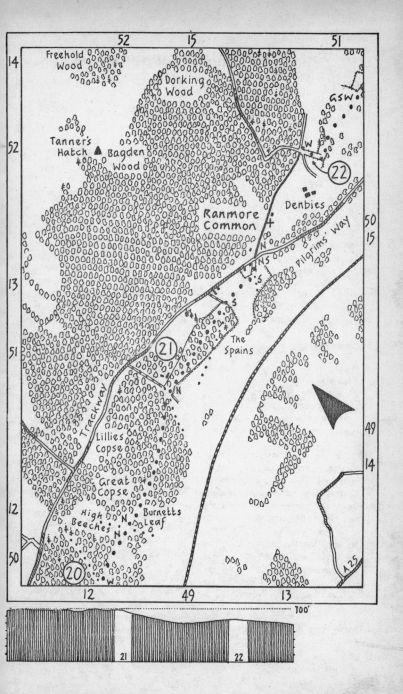

Freehold
Wood

Dorking
Wood

GSW

Tanner's
Hatch
Bagden
Wood

W

22

Denbies

Ranmore
Common

N

Pilgrims' Way

NS
S

21

S

The
Spains

N

Trackway

Lillies
Copse

Great
Copse

High
Beeches
N
Burnetts
Leaf

N

20

A 25

100'

21

22

52   15   51   14   52   13   51   50   15   49   14   50   12   49   13

10. Ashcombe Wood, Box Hill, Brockham Hills

2¾ miles
Maps: 1:25000 sheet TQ15; 1:50000 sheet 187

East-bound: Continue following the carriageway from Denbies – it bears sharply right at mile 23 and then passes under the railway. Take great care crossing the busy A24 (better to use the subway a little to the north). Walk to the stepping stones but if the river is too high follow the bank to the footbridge. Now climb the very steep route up Box Hill and take the path which runs parallel to the road to Upper Boxhill Farm. Leave the road at the café and follow the path alongside a fence behind a caravan site.

West-bound: From Brockham Hills the path follows the fence behind the caravan site and then goes up some steps near a café to run parallel to the road. Where the road bears sharply right the path goes forward down the very steep slope of Box Hill to the river. Cross by the stepping stones (if the river is in flood walk to your right to the footbridge). Continue forward from the stepping stones until reaching the busy A24, cross with great care (preferably using the subway to the north), take the track opposite which runs under the railway and then sweeps round to the left, climbing up through Ashcombe Wood.

The stepping stones over the Mole were a gift of the Rt Hon. Chuter Ede, Home Secretary during the first post-war Labour administration and a great friend of ramblers. The footbridge was given by the Southern Area of the Ramblers Association as a tribute to those who died in the war. Box Hill is probably the most popular of all the Surrey beauty spots, visited, particularly at weekends, by hordes of people. The steep path up the hill from the River Mole is very badly eroded. Before it became popular, it must have been an attractive spot and it has a number of literary and historical associations. At the Burford Bridge Hotel, Keats wrote part of *Endymion* and Lord Nelson made his last farewell to Lady Hamilton. George Meredith, the Victorian poet and novelist, lived for many years at Flint Cottage and set the scenes of some of his novels in the country around Box Hill.

Dorking, 1 mile off the Path, has a population of 23,000 and a bus service to Box Hill, Brighton, Chilworth, Crawley, Croydon, Ewhurst, Gomshall, Guildford, Horsham, Kingston, Leatherhead, London, Ranmore, Redhill, Reigate and Shere. There are three railway stations in Dorking. From Deepdene and Dorking Town there are services to Reading, Guildford, Chilworth, Gomshall, Redhill, Edenbridge and Ton-

continued on p. 48

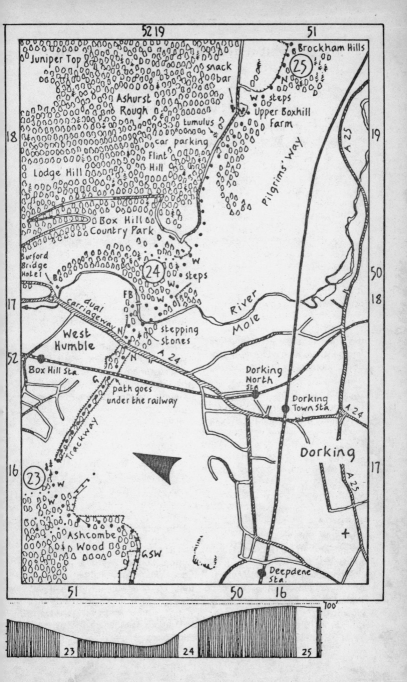

52 19   51

Brockham Hills

Juniper Top

snack bar

Ashurst Rough

25

N W steps

Upper Boxhill Farm

Tumulus

18   19

car parking

Flint Hill

Lodge Hill

Pilgrims' Way

A 25

Box Hill Country Park

Burford Bridge Hotel

24

W steps

50

17   18

dual carriageway

W FB W

River Mole

West Humble

N stepping stones

N

A 24

52

Box Hill Sta.

Dorking North Sta.

Dorking Town Sta.

A 24

path goes under the railway

Dorking

Trackway

16   17

23

W

A 25

Ashcombe Wood

GSW

Deepdene Sta.

51   50   16

100'

23   24   25

11. Brockham Hills, Pebblehill, Lady Hill

3 miles
Maps: 1:25000 sheets TQ15 and TQ25; 1:50000 sheet 187

East-bound: At point A walkers must continue forward at the hairpin bend down some steps to a wide track. Turn left and follow the track, which then drops down to the right and passes through some old chalk quarries to reach an unmade road. Turn right, walk to the main road, turn left and follow the pavement to Hazelcombe, where the footway continues along the bank above the road. Where the path rejoins the road cross the road and walk down an enclosed path to Bridlecombe Barn. Turn left across a stile and follow the field edge to the wood, ignore a right-hand fork and continue with a fence on your right, keeping to the foot of the hill.

West-bound: Follow the fence which keeps to the foot of the hills and then cross a field to reach Bridlecombe Barn at a gate and stile. Turn right, follow the enclosed path to Pebblehill Road, cross the road and turn left along the path which runs above the road. Turn right at Betchworth Lodge and shortly left along an unmade road, and take the path which 100 yds later turns off to the left. Follow this through the chalk quarries and, where it starts to go steeply downhill, look for the steps on the right which lead up to a hairpin bend.

Just above the path at point B is the grave of Quick, 'an English thoroughbred 26.9.36–22.10.44'.

The Betchworth chalk quarries have probably been worked for centuries and may even date from prehistoric times, when early man required the flint to construct his tools.

---

continued from p. 46
bridge and from Dorking North trains to Leatherhead, Epsom, Sutton, London Victoria, Wimbledon, Clapham Junction, London Waterloo and Horsham. Early closing day in Dorking is Wednesday. From Box Hill station near West Humble there are train services to Leatherhead, Epsom, Sutton, London Victoria, Raynes Park, Wimbledon, Clapham Junction, London Waterloo, Dorking and Horsham. From the Burford Bridge Hotel there are bus services to Dorking, Leatherhead, Ashtead and Epsom.

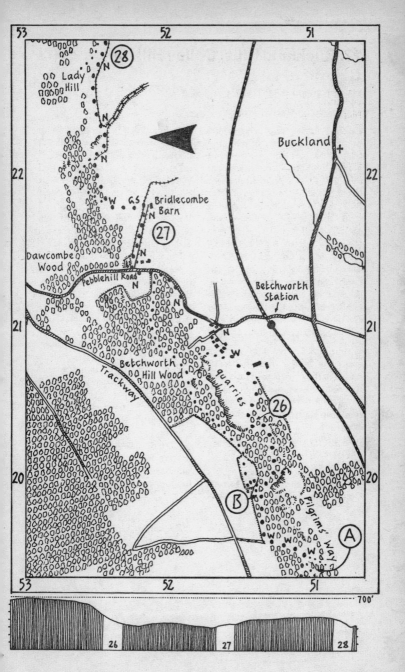

53 · 52 · 51

28

Lady
Hill

22

Buckland +

22

W G.S
Bridlecombe
N Barn

27

Dawcombe
Wood

Pebblehill Road N

N

N

Betchworth
Station

21

N

21

W

Betchworth
Hill Wood

Trackway

quarries

26

20

B

20

Pilgrims' Way

A

W W W

53 · 52 · 51

700'

26 · 27 · 28

12. Buckland Hills, Colley Hill, Reigate Hill

3 miles
Maps: 1:25000 sheet TQ25; 1:50000 sheet 187

East-bound: Follow the fence from Buckland Hills around the base of Juniper Hill until reaching a major junction of tracks near mile 29. At this point turn sharp left and walk very steeply uphill for 300 yds. On reaching the metalled road, turn right and follow the path over Colley Hill, past the tempietta and the water tower to a bridge which crosses the A217. This will bring you into the car park on the top of Reigate Hill, where there are toilets and a snack bar. Continue to the far end of the car park, cross the lane and you will see a path continuing ahead.

West-bound: From the car park cross the bridge over the A217 and take the track which runs past the water tower and tempietta on Colley Hill. On reaching a metalled road turn sharp left down the very steep hill to a junction of tracks near the bottom. Turn right and follow a path, keeping a fence on your left.

The tempietta on the top of Colley Hill is a charming little building which has suffered much in recent years from vandals. It houses a drinking fountain, which no longer works. It was presented by Lieutenant-Colonel Robert William Inglis, T.D., in 1909 to the Corporation of the Borough of Reigate for the benefit of the public. It has a charming mosaic ceiling representing the hours.

Reigate, 1 mile off the Path, has a population of 55,000. There are bus services to Betchworth, Brighton, Caterham, Coulsdon, Crawley, Croydon, Dorking, East Grinstead, Epsom, Gatwick, Godstone, Heathrow, Horley, Kingston, Luton, Merstham, Purley, Redhill, St Albans, Surbiton, Sutton, Tolworth, Uxbridge and Westerham and train services to Reading, Guildford, Shalford, Chilworth, Gomshall, Dorking, Betchworth, Redhill, Godstone, Edenbridge and Tonbridge. Early closing day is Wednesday.

From Reigate Hill there are bus services to Kingston, Epsom, Reigate and Redhill.

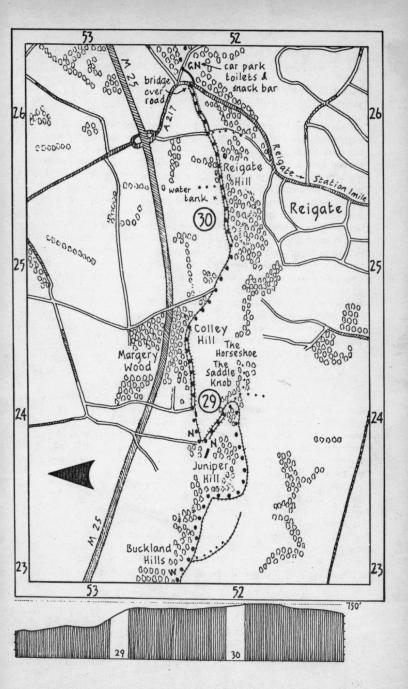

13. Wingate Hill, Gatton Hall, Merstham

3 miles
Maps: 1:25000 sheet TQ25; 1:50000 sheet 187

East-bound: From the car park on Reigate Hill take the path which goes through the trees and joins the road near a crossroads. Turn right and follow a road through the grounds of Gatton Park, past Gatton Hall, to reach another road. Turn right at the road and then turn left past White Hall Farm down a lane which leads into a field at a stile. Follow the fence on your left, then cross a large field to reach a stile near a playing field and continue up the side of the playing field into the village of Merstham. Turn left along Quality Street and at the end turn right and follow the metalled path over the M25 to reach a road. Turn right, cross the A23 at a staggered road junction and continue forward for ¼ mile.

West-bound: Continue down the road until reaching the A23 at a staggered road junction. Cross over and continue forward for 100 yds or so, looking for a metalled path on your left which crosses the motorway by a bridge and leads into Quality Street. Turn left down Quality Street and, just before reaching the main road at the bottom, turn right between some buildings and take the path which runs down beside the playing field to a stile. Continue across the large field walking parallel to the motorway and you will arrive at the stile which leads into a lane. Continue to the end of the lane, turn right and in a short distance turn left through the gates leading to Gatton Hall. On reaching the main buildings take the road that bears off to the right and follow it to the public road. Turn right and, just before reaching a crossroads, turn left along a track which runs parallel to a minor road. This will bring you to the car park on Reigate Hill.

Gatton Hall is now the Royal Alexandra and Albert School.

Merstham has a grocer's shop, open Sunday mornings, a post office, a bank, a public house, the Feathers, a café, buses to Croydon, Purley, Redhill, Horley, Gatwick, Crawley, Reigate, Dorking, Caterham and Woldingham and train services to London Victoria, East Croydon, Purley, Redhill, Salfords, Horley, Gatwick and Brighton.

Quality Street got its name when Seymour Hicks, the actor, and his wife Ellaline Terriss lived at the Old Forge House just before the First World War. They were appearing at the time in J. M. Barrie's famous play *Quality Street* and the name stuck.

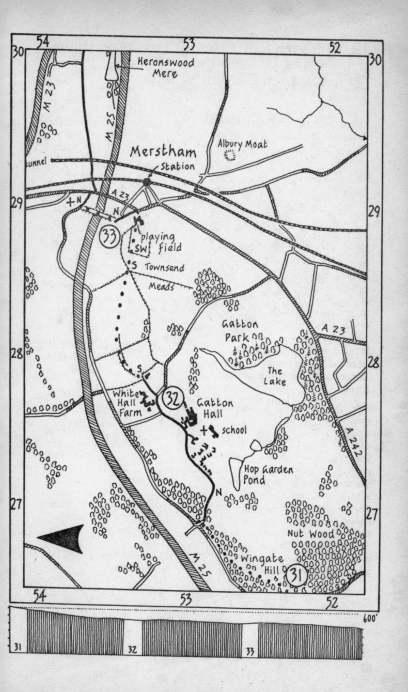

14. Ockley Hill, Willey Farm, War Coppice Garden Village

3 miles
Maps: 1:25000 sheet TQ35; 1:50000 sheet 187

East-bound: Turn left off the road by mile 34 and follow the edge of the field to a subway under the M23. Bear round to the right, then continue uphill across a couple of fields and through a gate to turn right along an enclosed track to reach the road. Continue forward to Willey Farm to join the road, take the right-hand road and follow it all the way to War Coppice Garden Village. Just beyond a crossroads turn right along the track which leaves the road.

West-bound: On arriving at the road continue forward over a crossroads, past a crossroads at Arthur's Seat, to Willey Farm, where the road turns sharp right. At this point take the track on the left past the tower and pond and Willey Farm and follow it for ½ mile to a road. Cross over and 300 yds later look for a gate on the left-hand side. Pass through this gate and then walk diagonally across a couple of fields to a road which passes under the motorway. Turn left immediately beyond the motorway and follow the edge of the field towards some houses at the road. At the road turn right.

The name Willey Farm is derived from the Old English *wille* or *willes*, which means either 'Willa's clearing' or possibly the 'clearing among the willows'.

Arthur's Seat is the name of a house and not as one might suppose, an earthwork. Cardinal's Cap is an Iron Age hill fort of univallate construction more than a third of a mile in diameter.

Whitehill Tower is a folly built in 1862 by Jeremiah Long.

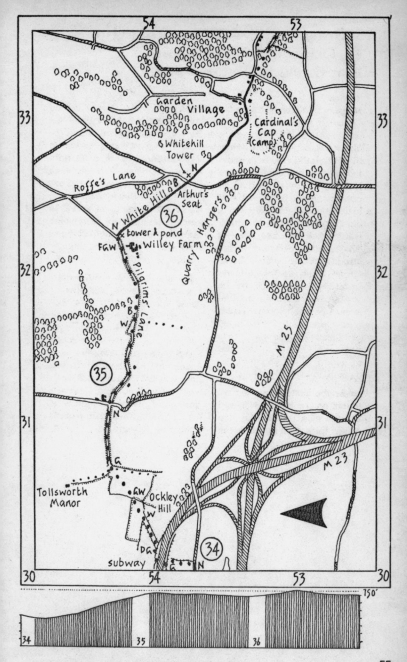

15. Gravelly Hill, A22, Tandridge Hill

2¾ miles
Maps: 1:25000 sheet TQ35; 1:50000 sheet 187

East-bound: Follow the track until it rejoins the road, turn right for a short distance and then turn right again off the road to follow a clear path through the woods to rejoin the road near a modern footbridge over the A22. Cross the bridge and continue forward over the first field which will bring you to a track. Turn right along this track and after a few yards bear left over a stile to reach a factory in the disused Godstone Quarries. Cross the road, continue forward and then follow a clear track. At the road by the entrance to the Convent of the Sacred Heart, continue on along an enclosed track to reach another road. Cross this and go forward to the next road, along which you turn left and climb up Tandridge Hill.

West-bound: Fork left at the road junction on Tandridge Hill and after ¼ mile, look for an enclosed track running off to the right. Follow this across a road and you will eventually arrive at a factory. Cross the road by the factory and continue ahead to reach an enclosed track, turn right and almost immediately left over a field to a footbridge which crosses the A22. Continue forward up the road for 100 yds or so and then turn left along a clear path which bears round to the right through some woods to rejoin the road. At the road turn left.

Godstone, 1 mile off the Path, has a grocer's shop, post office, a bank, a café, a restaurant, bus services to Croydon, Purley, Caterham, East Grinstead, Reigate, Redhill, Oxted, Westerham and Bromley and train services to Edenbridge, Tonbridge, Redhill, Reigate, Dorking, Gomshall, Chilworth, Guildford and Reading. Note that Godstone station is on the A22 about 2 miles south of the village.

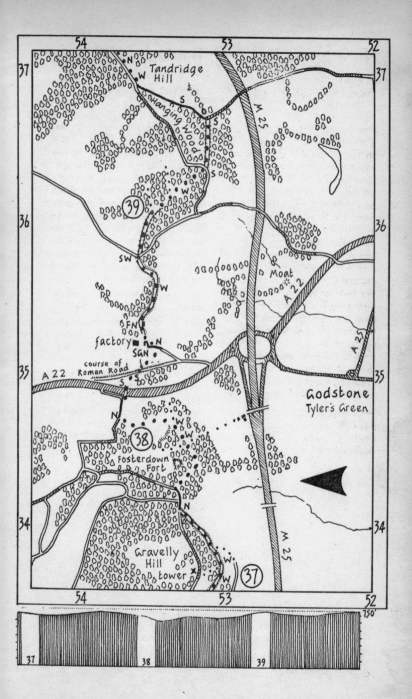

Tandridge
Hill

Hanging Wood

M 25

39

Moat

A 22

A 25

FN
factory
SGN
course of Roman Road
A 22

Godstone
Tyler's Green

38
Fosterdown
Fort

N

Gravelly
Hill
tower
37

M 25

54   53   52

37   38   39

150'

16. Tandridge Hill, Botley Hill, Titsey Park

3 miles
Maps: 1:25000 TQ35; 1:50000 sheet 187

East-bound: The Path runs beside the road on the right-hand side. Where the road bears to the left, immediately above the railway tunnel, turn right to go down some steps and then bear left over a stile and follow the hillside for about $\frac{1}{4}$ mile before turning right down the hill. Turn left and follow the fence to Chalkpit Lane. Cross over to a stile and continue forward over a field. Follow the edge of Titsey Plantation to a hollow way and then turn left to reach a road junction. At the road junction continue forward and you will find a path which turns to the right and follows the lower road.

West-bound: Follow the path alongside the road until reaching a road junction. At this point turn left, cross the road and walk down a hollow way for about $\frac{1}{4}$ mile; then turn right over a stile and walk along the edge of Titsey Plantation. Continue forward, cross Chalkpit Lane, follow the fence on your right and then turn right up the hill and then left again to reach some steps at a road. Turn left and follow the road.

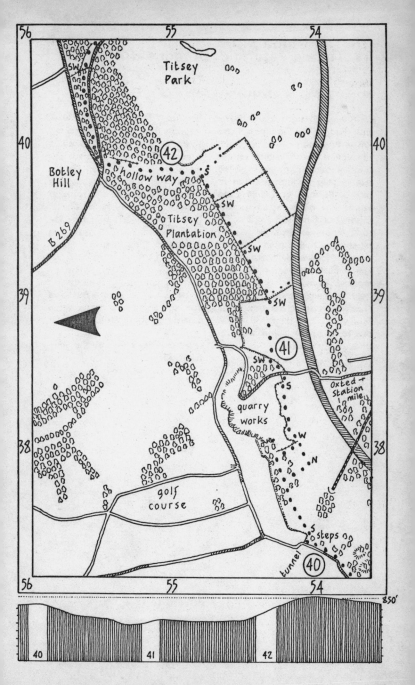

56   55   54

SW

Titsey Park

42

Botley Hill

hollow way   S

SW

Titsey Plantation

B 269

SW

SW

41

SW

Oxted → Station 1 mile

S

quarry works

W

N

golf course

steps

tunnel   40

56   55   54

40   39   40

39   39

38   38

850'

40   41   42

17. Titsey, Tatsfield, Betsons Hill, A233

$2\frac{1}{2}$ miles
Maps: 1:25000 sheet TQ45/55: 1:50000 sheet 187

East-bound: The Path turns sharp left at a picnic table to leave the road and very shortly cross another road. Continue forward over a stile through a wood to reach the road at Clarks Lane Farm. The Path actually runs inside the field and rejoins the road at some steps by a road junction. At the road junction continue forward along a metalled lane which bifurcates the two roads. This will bring you to a road, where you should turn right and follow it across the Kent/Surrey border to the A233. Cross this road, turn left and walk up through the woods.

West-bound: Come down through the woods to reach the A233. Cross this road and follow a lane which runs through the woods, crosses the Kent/Surrey border and, where it bends very sharply round to the right, turn off to the left along a lane which will bring you to a road junction. At the road junction turn left, go down some steps and almost immediately right to walk parallel to the B2024 road. At Clarks Lane Farm turn off left across a couple of fields to a wood, cross a road and you will arrive at a picnic table where you should turn right and walk through the wood, almost touching the road on the left-hand side.

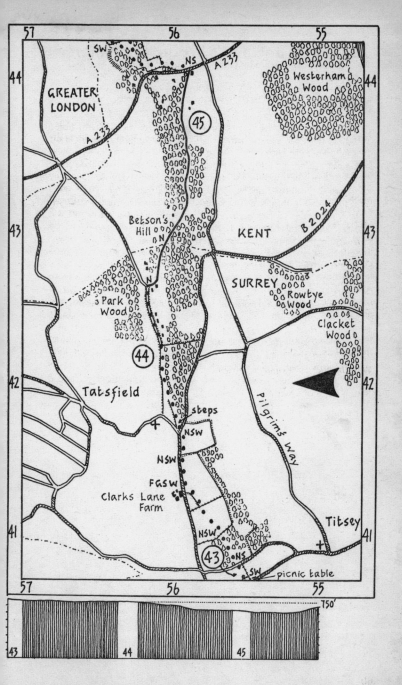

18. A233, Joeland's Wood, Knockholt

2½ miles
Maps: 1:25000 sheet TQ45/55; 1:50000 sheets 187 and 188

East-bound: After crossing the A233, the Path bears to the left and then right through a wood, keeping a fence on the left-hand side. An enclosed path soon comes in from the right, at a stile waymarked with a North Downs Way sign. *Be sure not to cross the next stile* but turn right and, keeping the fence on your left-hand side, walk almost to the road and then turn left over a stile and walk along the field edge parallel to the road. Cross over the next road and continue forward across a field, which will bring you to another road. Continue forward, keeping just inside the field edge following the road on the left. Where the road bears sharply to the left continue forward along the edge of a wood, turn left and then right after the trig point, to arrive at a road near Knockholt.

West-bound: Leave the road near Knockholt at a North Downs Way sign. Cross a stile, turn left and then right at the edge of the wood. Continue forward to reach a road and then bear left to walk parallel to the road, keeping to the field edge, to arrive at a road junction near Stoneings and then go straight on over the road to reach another road. The Path then continues forward keeping to the field edge with the road on its left-hand side. At the second fence be sure to turn right and walk up towards Joeland's Wood. On reaching the wood turn left, keeping inside the field, and then follow the waymarks to the A233.

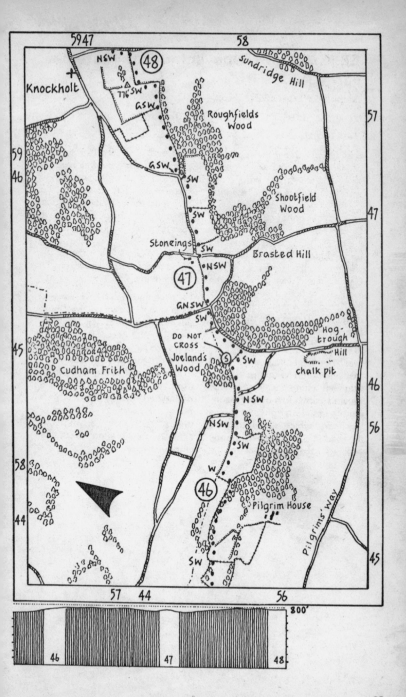

19. Knockholt, Chevening Park, Turvin's Farm, A2028

3 miles
Maps: 1:25000 sheet TQ45/55; 1:50000 sheet 188

East-bound: Cross the road near Knockholt and follow a series of stiles and waymarks around the wood on the edge of Chevening Park. (On one of these stiles if you look to your right you will see the famous keyhole view of Chevening House.) On reaching the road, turn right for a few yards and then left across a field to reach a wood. Bear right and walk parallel to the road and, where it bears sharply left, drop downhill, following a hedge, to Turvin's Farm. At the farm turn left along the B2211 and then right along the A2028.

West-bound: Follow the A2028 to its junction with the B2211, turn left and walk towards Turvin's Farm. Just before reaching the farm turn right and follow the hedge which almost touches the road at Star House. Continue walking roughly parallel to the road and then bear off left through a wood to reach another road. At the road turn right and almost immediately left over a stile, following the edge of the wood. (On one of the stiles, if you look to your left, you will see the famous keyhole view of Chevening House.) Follow the edge of the wood and then bear left to reach the road near Knockholt.

Chevening House is said to have been designed by Inigo Jones. When the Earl of Stanhope died in 1967 he bequeathed the house, together with $3\frac{1}{2}$ thousand acres of land and the sum of $\frac{1}{4}$ million pounds, to the nation to be used as a home for certain designated people. In 1974 it became the home of the Prince of Wales, but after carrying out extensive restoration work he relinquished it.

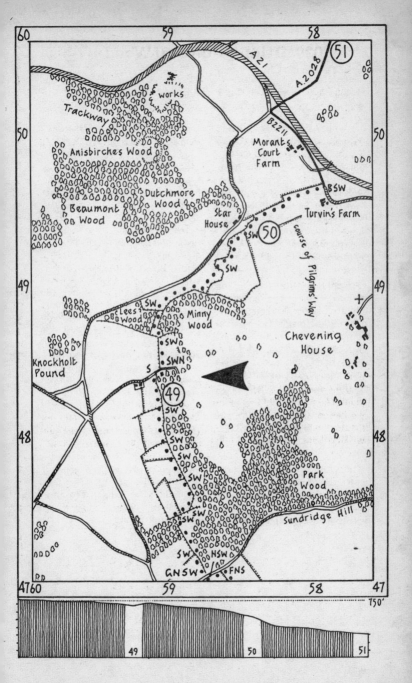

20. A2028, Otford, Hillydeal Wood

3 miles
Maps: 1:25000 sheet TQ45/55; 1:50000 sheet 188

East-bound: Follow the A2028 to a T-junction, turn left for a couple of hundred yards and then turn right across the edge of Donnington Manor Hotel. Continue forward across some fields to the railway, where the route becomes metalled all the way into Otford. Pass Otford railway station, turn right along Pilgrims' Way for 100 yds and then left up an enclosed path.

West-bound: Drop down the enclosed Path to the road, turn right and almost immediately left to follow the main road past the railway station into Otford. Continue straight ahead, past the village pond, and about $\frac{1}{4}$ mile after crossing the river turn left along a road which peters out at the railway. Cross the bridge and continue forward to the A2028 near Donnington Manor Hotel. Turn left along the main road and after 100 yds turn right.

Otford has a grocer's shop, open 6 days a week, a post office, a bank, several public houses, including the Rising Sun, buses to Sevenoaks, Kemsing, Westerham, Biggin Hill and Bromley. There are train services to Swanley, St Mary Cray, Bromley, London Victoria, Shoreham, Eynsford, London Blackfriars, Holborn Viaduct, Sevenoaks, Kemsing, Borough Green, West Malling and Maidstone East.

The parish church has a Norman tower and some attractive monuments and woodwork. Just to the south is an octagonal tower, which is virtually all that is left of the palace of Otford, once the residence of the Archbishops of Canterbury. Henry VIII stayed here on his way to the Field of the Cloth of Gold and coveted it, but in the end he preferred Knole and it became the residence of Princess Mary. Soon after the King's death the roof was stripped of its lead and very little now remains. Thomas à Becket stayed at Otford Castle and legend has it that he once cursed the nightingales for intruding upon his prayers. He is also reputed to have been responsible for the spring near the octagonal tower, which he caused to gush forth water by striking his staff on the ground.

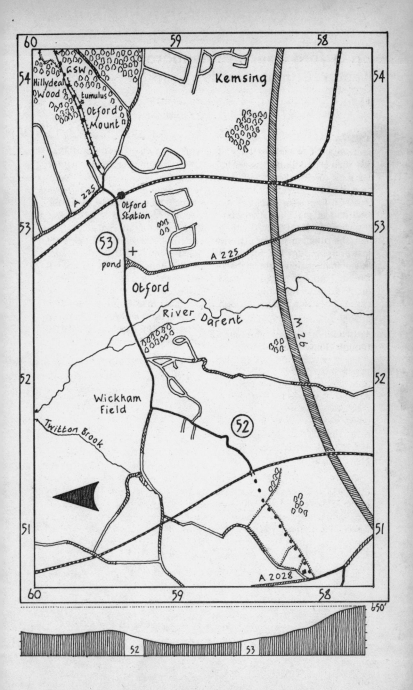

21. Otford Court, Hildenborough Hall, Kester, Summeryards Wood

3 miles
Maps: 1:25000 sheet TQ45/55; 1:50000 sheet 188

East-bound: On reaching the road near mile 54, continue forward for a couple of hundred yards and then bear off to the right to reach Shorehill Farm. Turn right at the road and at the T-junction continue forward for 100 yds and then turn sharp left to follow a fence past a cross. Turn left again and almost immediately right to reach a road. Turn left along the road and 75 yds later turn right to cross a couple of fields and go through a wood.

West-bound: Follow the fence through Summeryards Wood, on reaching a road turn left and after 100 yds turn right, following the hillside. Turn sharp left near Hildenborough Hall, turn right at the next stile, walk past the cross and re-join the road. Walk along the road for a few yards and then continue across several fields to reach another road. Turn left and at the road junction continue forward and drop down into Otford. Be sure to fork left at the stile near mile 55 otherwise you will end up at the Youth Hostel in Kemsing. The more obvious path runs steeply downhill.

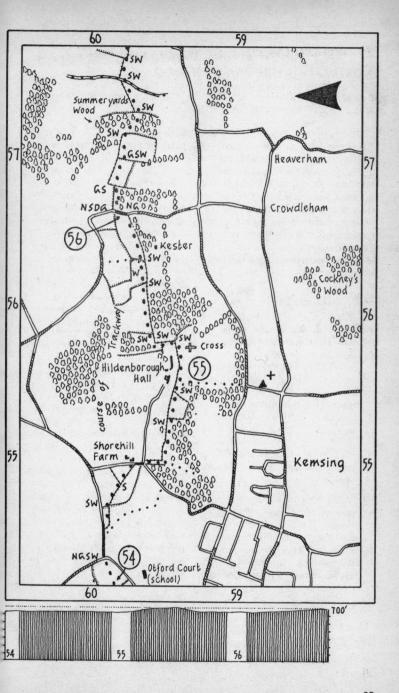

Summer yards
Wood

Heaverham

Crowdleham

Kester

Cockney's
Wood

Trackway

Cross

Hildenborough
Hall

Kemsing

course of

Shorehill
Farm

Otford Court
(school)

60   59

57   57

56   56

55   55

56

55

54

SW
SW
SW
SW
GSW
GS
NSDG NG
W
SW
SW
SW SW
SW SW
SW
SW
S
SW
NGSW

700'

54   55   56

22. Chalk Pit Wood, White Hill, Wrotham

2½ miles
Maps: 1:25000 sheets TQ45/55 and TQ65/75; 1:50000 sheet 188

East-bound: On reaching the road at the edge of Chalk Pit Wood cross over and go steeply downhill to reach a road at a sharp bend. Turn left and take the enclosed track which runs for a couple of miles into the outskirts of Wrotham. On reaching the main road turn right, then shortly left and follow a metalled lane which runs alongside the M20 and reaches a roundabout.

West-bound: Leave the roundabout and take the metalled lane that runs roughly parallel to the M20. On reaching the main road turn right and then shortly left down a minor road. At the end of this road the metalling ceases and the route becomes an enclosed track. Continue forward across a road to reach a second road on a very sharp right-angled corner. At this point turn right and walk uphill to reach another road, cross over, bearing slightly left, and follow the path up to Chalk Pit Wood.

Wrotham has a grocer's shop, a post office, a bank, three public houses, the George and Dragon, the Rose and Crown, and the Three Post Boys, and there are bus services to Gravesend, Vigo, Trosley Country Park, Borough Green, Maidstone, and Sevenoaks. Early closing day is Wednesday.

St George, the parish church of Wrotham, stands on a slight hill and is built on a Saxon site, although the present church dates from the thirteenth century. The tower was built in the fifteenth century and is unusual in that it has an arch in it so that church processions could circle the church without leaving consecrated ground. In the arch is a stone with a number of little crosses which some say may have been scratched by crusaders going to the Holy Land or by pilgrims on their way to Canterbury. There are some good brasses and monuments and an interesting nuns' gallery which runs across the whole width of the church above the chancel arch. Nobody is quite sure of the purpose of this unusual feature, but it may possibly have been a watching chamber or have once housed a relic. Near the church is all that remains of the Archbishop's palace, which was demolished by Archbishop Simon Islip in the middle of the fourteenth century to provide building material for his new palace at Maidstone.

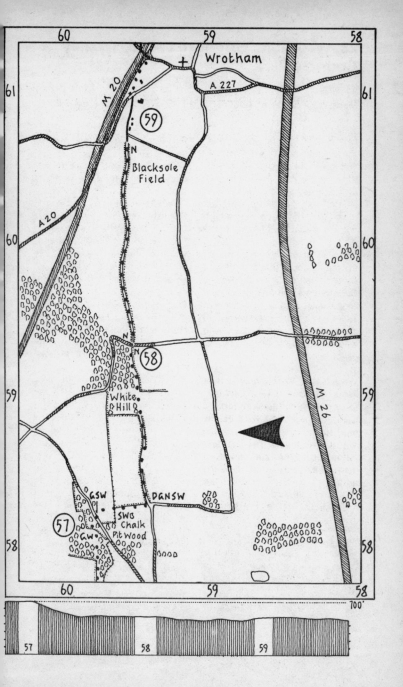

Wrotham

A 227

M 20

(59)

N
Blacksole
Field

A 20

N
N
(58)

White
Hill

M 26

GSW
DGNSW
SWG
(57)
GW
Chalk
Pit Wood

700'

57   58   59

23. Wrotham, Hognore Wood, Trosley Country Park

$3\frac{1}{4}$ miles

Maps: 1:25000 sheets TQ65/75 and TQ66/76; 1:50000 sheet 188

East-bound: Cross the roundabout on the outskirts of Wrotham and take the metalled Pilgrims' Way. At the road junction about 300 yds beyond Hognore Farm, bear left off the road up through the edge of the wood, past a high brick wall to a road junction near the Vigo public house. Turn right and walk down the lane, keeping the public house on your left, and shortly bear off left into Trosley Country Park and follow the clear broad track through the woods. There is a complicated system of waymarks for those who want short strolls in the country park.

West-bound: Walk through Great Wood and Downs Wood, following a clear broad track to reach a road, turn right and walk up the road to the road junction at the Vigo public house. Turn left and follow a path through the woods past a high wall to arrive at the bottom of the hill at a road. Turn right and follow this road to the roundabout on the outskirts of Wrotham.

Behind the brick wall, near mile 61 in Hognore Wood, are the remains of Trosley Towers, destroyed by fire before the Second World War and once the home of Sir Sydney Waterlow, founder of the famous Waterlow printing company.

The Vigo public house gets its unusual name from the Battle of Vigo (1702), when an Anglo-Dutch fleet destroyed the Franco-Spanish fleet sheltering in Vigo Bay off the north-west coast of Spain, capturing 1 million pounds worth of treasure. As usual, the prize money was shared out among the fleet and one sailor built this pub on his proceeds. Prize money was one of the few ways in which humble sailors could earn undreamed of wealth.

Trosley Country Park has a large car park, toilets and a visitors' centre.

The village of Trottiscliffe, pronounced Trosley, lies a mile off the path at the foot of the Downs. It is a pleasant spot and was once the home of the painter Graham Sutherland, whose famous portrait of Sir Winston Churchill was destroyed by Lady Churchill and who designed the tapestry in Coventry Cathedral. The parish church, originally Saxon, was largely rebuilt by the Normans. The enormous pulpit was designed for Westminster Abbey.

Trottiscliffe has a post office stores (half-day closing Wednesday and Saturday), two public houses and bus services to Maidstone and Borough Green.

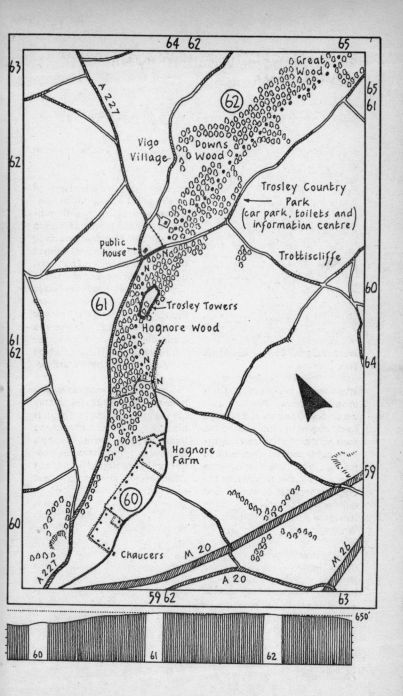

24. Whitehorse Wood, Holly Hill, Greatpark Wood

2½ miles
Maps: 1:25000 sheet TQ66/76; 1:50000 sheet 188 or 178

East-bound: On reaching the fence go through the kissing gate and turn right to follow the edge of the wood along a clearly defined trackway. Beyond the wood it becomes enclosed. Just before it bends sharply right, look for a stile on the left-hand side which goes across a field and up the hill. On reaching the road continue forward along a road past a car park on your left. Where the metalling ceases, bear slightly right and walk along the edge of a wood and then into Greatpark Wood.

West-bound: From Greatpark Wood follow the clearly defined path to a metalled lane, turn left and walk to a T-junction. Continue along the path opposite which goes downhill and across a field to meet an enclosed track. Turn right along the track, ignoring another track which runs off to the left, and continue into the edge of Whitehorse Wood. On meeting the end of a metalled road bear right and follow the fence to turn left at a kissing gate.

Where the path touches the end of a metalled lane and then turns left, near mile 63, a path runs across the field to what is marked on the 1:25000 Ordnance Survey map as a long barrow belonging to the National Trust. This long barrow is usually known as the Coldrum Stones. It was excavated in 1910 and 22 skeletons were found, together with the bones of ox, deer, rabbit, cat and fox. The burial chamber was constructed from huge sarsen stones (which must have come from a considerable distance as there are none locally) and then covered with a huge mound of earth, leaving only the entrance accessible. The best examples of such chambered tombs are to be seen at Wayland's Smithy on the Ridgeway Path, not far from White Horse Hill, and the West Kennett long barrow near Avebury.

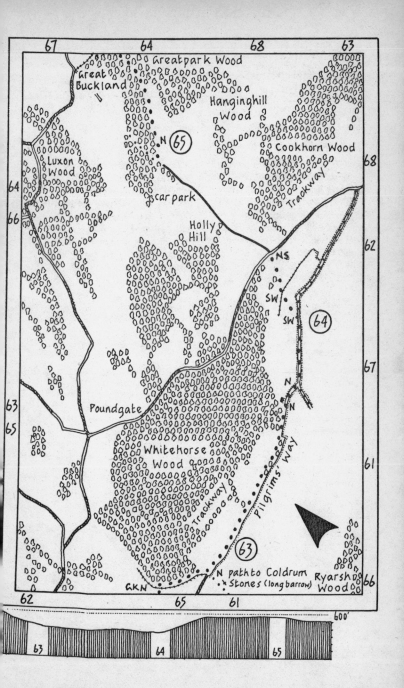

25. Greatpark Wood, Pastead Wood, Upper Bush

2½ miles
Maps: 1:25000 sheet TQ66/76; 1:50000 sheet 178

East-bound: Continue through Greatpark Wood and cross the clearing into Horseholders Wood and past a scout hut. The route is quite clear throughout the wood and is well waymarked but be sure to bear left at The Warren in order to reach the road at Upper Bush.

West-bound: Where the road ends continue forward along a path which takes you into North Wood and on to the next wood, The Warren. Bear right at this point and continue along a well waymarked path to a scout hut, just beyond which is a clearing which leads into Greatpark Wood.

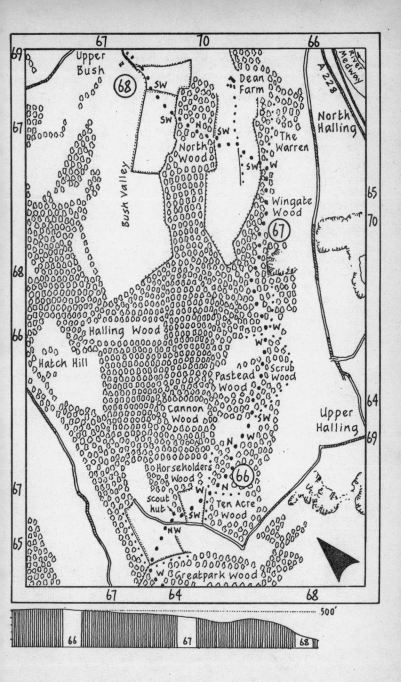

67 70 66

69 Upper Bush
68
SW
SW
N
North Wood
SW
Dean Farm
North Halling
The Warren
SW W

67

Bush Valley

65 70
Wingate Wood
67

68

66 Halling Wood
W
W
W
Scrub Wood
Hatch Hill
Pastead Wood
64
Cannon Wood
SW
W
Upper Halling
69
N
Horseholders Wood
66
N
67 W N
scout hut
SW
Ten Acre Wood
NW
65
W Greatpark Wood

67 64 68

500'

66 67 68

26. Upper Bush, Medway Bridge

3 miles
Maps: 1:25000 sheet TQ66/76; 1:50000 sheet 178

East-bound: From Upper Bush follow the road towards Lower Bush. Where it turns very sharply left, strike out across the field to cut off the corner. Turn right along the road for a few yards and then left again beside a fence with a housing estate on your right. Turn left over the railway and continue forward through a gap and walk up the hill following the edge of a wood. Bear right following the line of trees and then turn sharp right along a farm track to the A228. Turn left and then right across the footway alongside the motorway over the Medway and on the far side turn right and descend to the road below. Turn left and follow the road that runs exactly parallel to, but below, the M2.

West-bound: On reaching the T-junction turn right and climb up to the pedestrian footway over the Medway bridge. On the far side of the Medway turn left along the A228 and, a couple of hundred yards later, turn right along an access road leading to Ranscombe Farm. At first it is metalled but it soon deteriorates to a track. Turn left off this track, follow a fence and then bear left round the edge of a wood to cross the bridge over a railway. Turn right on the far side of the railway and follow a clear path to the road. At the road go straight on across a field to reach a road and continue forward down the road to Upper Bush.

Cuxton has a grocer's shop, a post office, public houses, bus services to Gillingham, Rochester, Maidstone and Snodland and trains to Paddock Wood, Maidstone, Strood and London Charing Cross. Early closing day is Wednesday.

Rochester has a population of 55,000. Early closing day is Wednesday. There are bus services to Caxton, Snodland, Maidstone, Chatham, Gravesend and Dartford, and rail services to Gillingham, Sittingbourne, Dover, Margate, Ramsgate, Gravesend, London Charing Cross and London Victoria. (There is a Tourist Information Centre, 85 High Street (tel. Medway 43666).) (*For a description of Rochester see p. 143.*)

The noise from traffic on the Medway bridge is deafening and tends to detract from the interesting views. To the left is Fort Borstal, built as a defence against a possible invasion by Napoleon. The village of Borstal gave its name to the detention centres set up for young people.

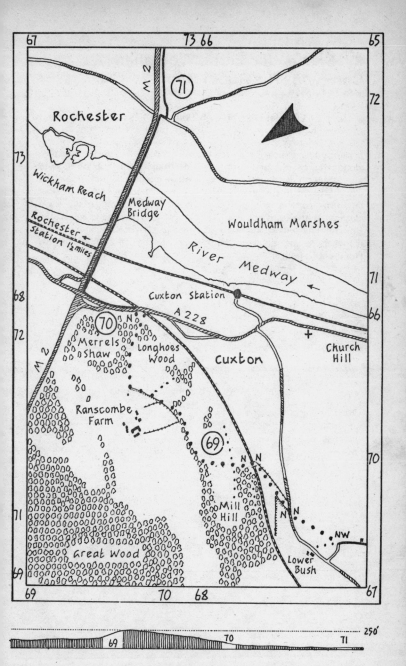

Rochester

M 2

71

72

Wickham Reach

Medway
Bridge

Rochester ←
Station 1½miles

Wouldham Marshes

River Medway ←

71

Cuxton Station

A 228

66

70

N

Merrels
Shaw

Longhoes
Wood

Cuxton

Church
Hill

72

M 2

Ranscombe
Farm

69

N N

Mill
Hill

70

N N

71

Great Wood

N N

NW

Lower
Bush

69

69

70

68

61

250'

69

70

71

79

27. Nashenden Farm, Wouldham Common, The Robin Hood

$2\frac{1}{2}$ miles
Maps: 1:25000 sheet TQ66/76; 1:50000 sheet 178

East-bound: Follow the road alongside the M2 and turn off right through Nashenden Farm, passing between the farm buildings. The path is now perfectly clear all the way to the road at Burham Hill Farm. Continue along the road to the isolated Robin Hood public house.

West-bound: Follow the road past the Robin Hood public house to where it peters out at Burham Hill Farm and becomes a track. Follow this through the edge of the wood and on to Nashenden Farm. At the road just beyond the farm turn left and take the lane that runs parallel to, but below, the M2.

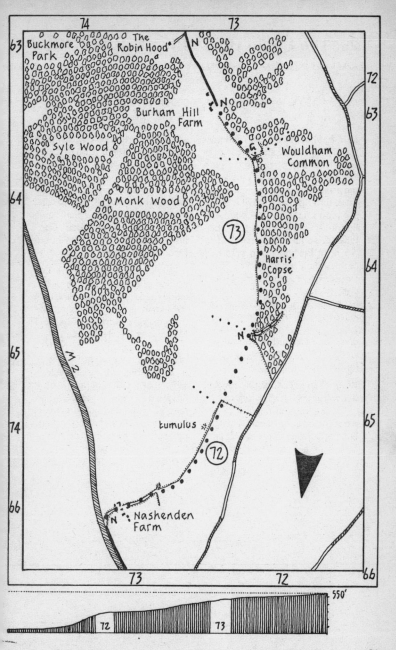

Buckmore
Park
The
Robin Hood
Burham Hill
Farm
Syle Wood
Monk Wood
Wouldham
Common
Harris'
Copse
⑺
tumulus
⑺
Nashenden
Farm

28. The Robin Hood, Blue Bell Hill, Kit's Coty House, Boarley Warren

$3\frac{1}{4}$ miles
Maps: 1:25000 sheet TQ66/76; 1:50000 sheet 188 or 178

East-bound: Follow the road past the Robin Hood. At the car park and picnic area on the right a path has been constructed parallel to the road. On reaching the A229 road, turn right and leave it at the slip road on the right. A couple of hundred yards down this road look for some steps going off to the right leading to an enclosed path which passes Kit's Coty House. On reaching a road junction, turn left along an enclosed track which runs underneath the A229. Ignore the enclosed track which runs off to the right and continue forward through the woods, bearing round to the right further on.

West-bound: Follow the edge of the wood and, just before reaching the road, turn left into the wood to reach an enclosed track which passes under the A229 and arrives at a road junction. Turn right uphill along an enclosed track, past Kit's Coty House, to some concrete steps which lead up to a slip road. Turn left and walk along the A229 to the cross-roads where there is a public house. Turn left and look for the path on the left which runs parallel to the road as far as the picnic area and then rejoins the road. Continue forward past the Robin Hood public house.

This is a particularly unattractive section of the route. Much of it is along roads and it is only near mile 77 that it is possible to escape from the roar of traffic. Kit's Coty House can clearly be seen from the path, enclosed with iron railings, with a path leading to it. It is a group of sarsen stones which is all that remains of a neolithic burial chamber, the mound of earth which once was heaped over it having disappeared. Another example of a burial chamber is the Countless Stones, a little to the south-east, just off the Path.

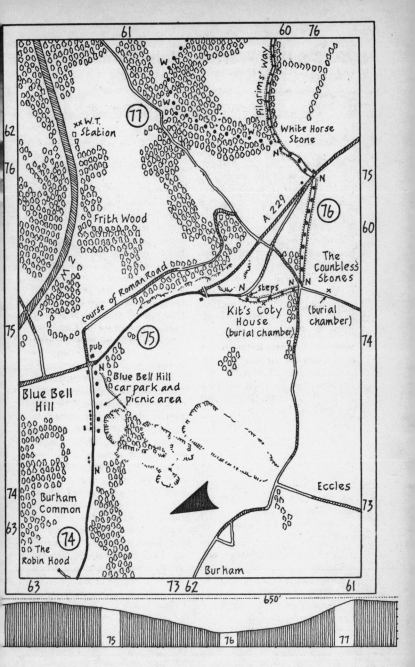

61   60 76

Pilgrims' Way

⑦

xx W.T. Station

White Horse Stone

N

62

76

A 229

⑦⑥

75

60

Frith Wood

The Countless Stones

course of Roman Road

steps

N   N

75

⑦⑤

N

pub

Kit's Coty House (burial chamber)

x
(burial chamber)

74

Blue Bell Hill car park and picnic area

N

Blue Bell Hill

Eccles

74

Burham Common

73

63

⑦④

The Robin Hood

Burham

63   73 62   61

650'

75   76   77

29. Boarley Warren, Harp Farm, Boxley Warren, A249

$3\frac{1}{4}$ miles
Maps: 1:25000 sheets TQ66/76 and TQ65/75; 1:50000 sheet 188 or 178

East-bound: Continue round the edge of the wood and, about 250 yds after entering it, turn left along a fence and then right to reach a road at Harp Farm. Continue forward, cross the next road and follow a clear track, keeping a fence on your left, to meet the next road. Here turn right and go steeply downhill to reach the A249. Turn right and walk down to the road junction, then turn left and follow the road past the Cock Horse Inn into Detling.

West-bound: Leave Detling by the road and walk up to the A249, cross it, turn right, follow it for 200 yds and then turn left to climb uphill along a path. On reaching the road at the top turn left to follow a clear track, keeping a fence on your right. On reaching a road continue forward to Harp Farm, cross another road, keeping a fence on your left, and then turn left, still following the fence. 200 yds later turn right through the wood and then follow the path which runs round the edge of the wood.

Boxley, $\frac{3}{4}$ mile off the path, is a small, attractive village with a pleasant pub and bus services to Chatham and Maidstone.

An unusual feature of Boxley church is the Norman porch, which once had an upper floor and a two-bayed north isle. It may have been a small mortuary chapel where bodies could lie before burial, or it may have housed a relic. Tennyson lived for a time at Park House. His sister Cecilia married Edmund Lushington and is buried in the Lady Chapel alongside other members of the Lushington family. The little stream which runs through Park House is probably the one described in Tennyson's poem *The Brook*.

A mile to the west lie the ruins of Boxley Abbey, originally a Cistercian house founded in 1146 and second only in importance to Waverley Abbey (see p. 28). The monks of Boxley Abbey owned a venerable cross which those seeking forgiveness for their sins had to lift after presenting their gifts. The monks devised a cunning locking device whereby the statue would only be released if the alms were sufficiently generous, when it would nod approvingly. The fraud was discovered at the Reformation and the statue was burned at St Paul's Cross.

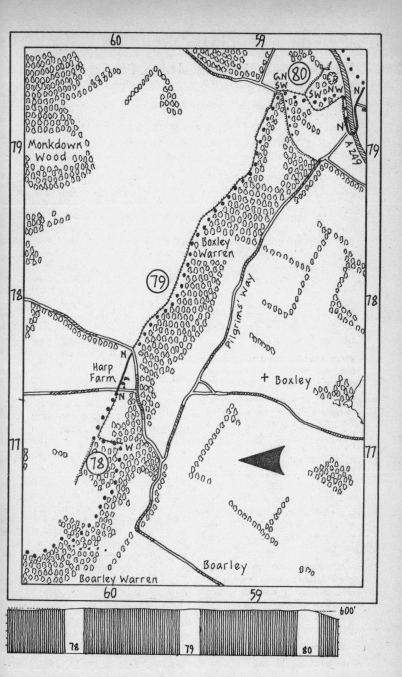

30. Detling, Thurnham, Whitehall

2¼ miles
Maps: 1:25000 sheets TQ65/75 and TQ85/95; 1:50000 sheet 188 or 178
The final route is shown but is not yet open.

East-bound: Walk down Detling High Street and take the enclosed lane which runs off left opposite the church. Cross a stile and a large field and walk through the edge of Thurnham churchyard. At the road turn left and take the farm road that runs off to the right, ignoring the forbidding notice on the telegraph pole. Where the road bears sharply left go forward across a field to a road, turn right for a short distance, then turn left through Cobham Oast House garden. Continue forward through a series of small fields and through the edge of the wood to arrive at the road beside Whitehall. Turn left, walk to the T-junction and turn right again.

West-bound: Turn left and follow the road to Whitehall, then turn right over the stile, cross a wood and go through some small paddocks to reach the road through Cobham Oast House garden. At the road turn right and, 50 yds later, turn left across the field to reach the farm road at Thurnham Keep Farm. Continue forward into Thurnham, at the T-junction turn left and then turn right through the edge of the churchyard. Continue forward across a large field to reach an enclosed path which runs between orchards to the road at Detling, opposite the church. Turn right and walk up the hill.

Detling has a grocer's shop, a post office stores, a public house, and buses to Maidstone, Sitting-bourne, Canterbury and Sheerness. Early closing: Wednesday.

The Norman parish church was considerably altered in the fourteenth and fifteenth centuries. It has a poor-box dug out of a solid tree trunk with the outline of a priest carved in stone, his hands clasped in prayer, and a splendid fourteenth-century lectern of superb craftsmanship and ingenuity, possibly from Boxley Abbey.

The Cockhorse Inn gets its name from the custom, in coaching days, of keeping a specially powerful horse, the cockhorse, to lead coaches up steep hills.

Thurnham has a public house. The parish church was probably built by the Normans but much of it dates from the thirteenth century. It has some brasses and a fine kingpost roof to the nave. In the churchyard is the grave of Alfred Mynn, the famous Kentish cricketer, and an unusual modern gravestone of a farmer and his wife containing in the headstone two old photographs of the couple. Opposite the Black Horse pub, just outside the village proper at the crossroads, is Thurnham Friars, a superb early-twentieth-century reproduction of a Tudor house. To the north of the crossroads lie the few remains of Thurnham Castle. In 1967 a Saxon gold cross set with polished garnets was discovered nearby.

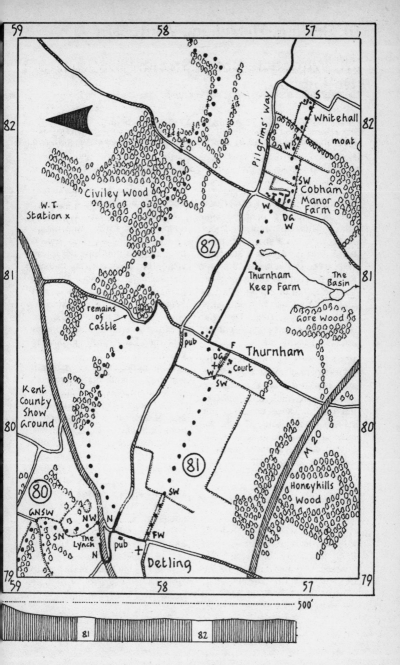

31. Whitehall, Broad Street, Hollingbourne

2½ miles

Maps: 1:25000 sheet TQ85/95; 1:50000 sheet 188 or 178

Note that maps 30 and 31 overlap very slightly between miles 82 and 83.

East-bound: Continue forward to the hamlet of Broad Street and turn left along a metalled lane which climbs up steeply. In about half a mile, on a sharp left-hand bend, turn right over a stile and walk through the woods, following for most of the way a fence on your left until dropping down to meet the road near Hollingbourne at the Pilgrims' Rest. Take the metalled lane, passing the pub on your right-hand side.

West-bound: On reaching the Pilgrims' Rest cross the B2163 and then turn right to take a narrow path which runs parallel to the road for a short time. It climbs steeply, then bears off left, for most of the way following a fence until it reaches a minor metalled lane on a sharp bend. Turn left, descend the lane to Broad Street and, at the T-junction, turn right and take the next turning on the left.

Walkers should note that the route on the road via Broad Street is a temporary diversion until access is negotiated along the top of the downs. The official route is shown but should not be used until such time as waymarks and signposts indicate that it is open.

Hollingbourne has a grocer's shop, a post office, two public houses, the Pilgrims' Rest beside the path and the Windmill in the village, bus services to Maidstone, Harrietsham, Lenham, Charing, Ashford, Sellindge, Hythe and Folkestone and train services to Harrietsham, Lenham, Charing, Ashford, Kemsing and London Victoria. Early closing day is Wednesday.

Hollingbourne is a linear village and most of it lies about a mile to the south of the path. The church dates from the fifteenth century and contains a considerable number of fine monuments to the Culpeper family, including one carved in alabaster showing a lady with a ring on her finger tied to a tape which disappears into her sleeve. In the chancel near the altar is a tomb of two couples kneeling above eight children. Near the church is a beautiful Elizabethan manor house built by the Culpepers and said to be haunted by the ghost of Catherine Howard, whose mother was a Culpeper.

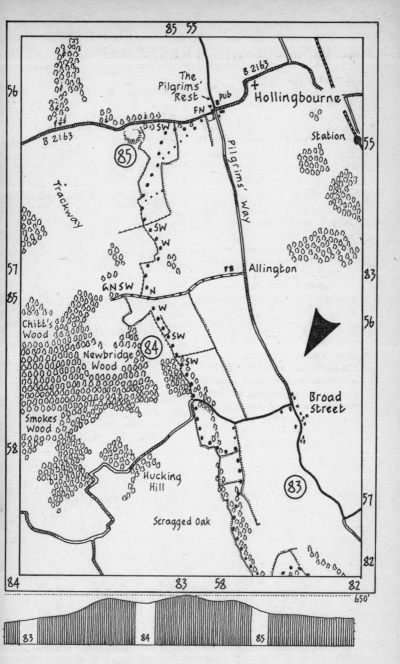

32. Hollingbourne, Harrietsham

2¾ miles
Maps: 1:25000 sheet TQ85/95: 1:50000 sheets 188 and 189

East-bound: Follow the metalled lane past the Pilgrims' Rest and continue forward when the metalling ceases. Near Hillside Farm the metalling starts again. Keep straight on.

West-bound: Follow the metalled lane until reaching the crossroads and continue forward to Hillside Farm, where the metalling ceases. Go on along an obvious track, which eventually arrives at a metalled lane on the outskirts of Hollingbourne. Continue forward.

Harrietsham has a grocer's shop open six days a week, a post office, three public houses, the Sugar Loaves, the Bank House and the Roebuck Inn, and a café on the main road. There are bus services to Maidstone, Hollingbourne, Lenham, Charing, Ashford, Sellindge, Hythe and Folkestone and trains to Lenham, Charing, Ashford, Hollingbourne, Maidstone, Kemsing and London Victoria.

Harrietsham is an attractive village but has suffered the misfortune of being cut in half by the A20. The parish church of St John the Baptist contains some Norman work and is peculiar in that it has two towers, one to the west dating from the fifteenth century and the other on the north side probably Norman and originally a two-storey sacristy. There is an unusual Norman font and some monuments to the Stede family, who lived at Stede Court. Edwin Stede ran his own cricket team and lost a great deal of money by betting on its fortunes.

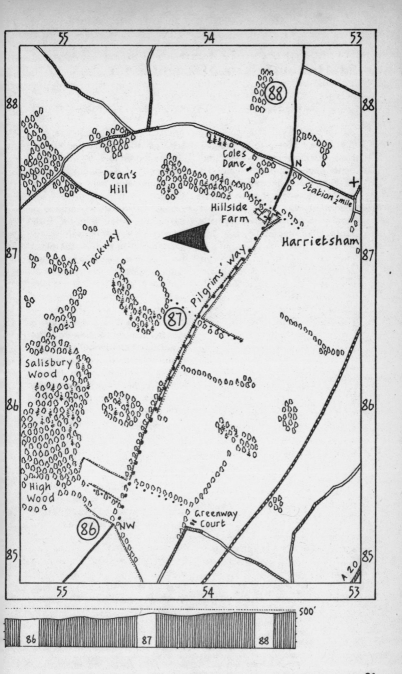

33. Marley Court, Lenham Chest Hospital

$2\frac{1}{4}$ miles
Maps: 1:25000 sheet TQ85/95; 1:50000 sheet 189

East-bound: Follow the road past the Marley Works to where the road makes a sharp right-hand bend, then go straight on along a track to reach another road. Go forward to where this road bears round to the right and then continue along a clear path which leads past some houses and through a gate to the Lenham war memorial. Continue forward across the field to reach an enclosed track and on to the road. Follow the road and where it bears round to the left keep straight on towards the Chest Hospital.

West-bound: After passing the Chest Hospital the track meets a road. Continue forward along the road and, where it makes a sharp left-hand bend, go on along another track which arrives at a field in front of the Lenham war memorial. Cross the field and pass some houses to the road, follow the road to where it bears sharply to the right and then leave it and follow a track which arrives at a road on a bend. Continue forward past Marley Court and the Marley Works.

The chalk cross is an attractive and unusual war memorial set in a splendid position overlooking the Weald of Kent.

Lenham, $\frac{3}{4}$ mile off the path, has a grocer's shop, several public houses, a bank, post office, bus services to Folkestone, Hythe, Sellindge, Ashford, Charing, Harrietsham, Hollingbourne and Maidstone and train services to Charing, Ashford, Harrietsham, Hollingbourne, Maidstone, Kemsing and London Victoria. Early closing day is Wednesday.

Lenham is a picturesque place built around the market square and contains an attractive collection of brick-faced and timber-framed buildings. The parish church of St Mary was built by the Normans on a Saxon site but it was burned down at the end of the thirteenth century and then rebuilt. There is a large tithe barn near the church which was burned down in the same fire and rebuilt at the same time. One of the curiosities of the church is the tomb of Mary Honywood in the chancel floor. She died in 1620 at the age of 92 and had 16 children, 114 grandchildren, 228 great-grandchildren and 9 great-great-grandchildren. She was a friend of John Foxe, the protestant hagiographer, whom she once told that she feared for her future at the day of judgement. She held a looking glass and said that she was as certain to be damned as the glass was to break, whereupon she dropped it and the looking glass remained unbroken.

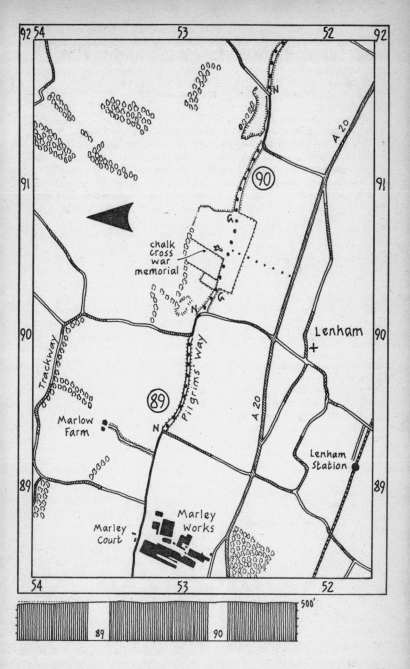

chalk
cross
war
memorial

Lenham

Lenham
Station

Trackway

Pilgrims Way

Marlow
Farm

Marley
Works

Marley
Court

A 20

500'

34. Lenham Chest Hospital, Charing Hill

2½ miles
Maps: 1:25000 sheet TQ85/95; 1:50000 sheet 189

East-bound: Continue past Lenham Chest Hospital following a clearly defined track to Hart Hill, turn right along the road for a few yards and then turn left along an enclosed trackway.

West-bound: From Charing Hill continue along the enclosed trackway to Hart Hill, turn right for a few yards and then turn left along another enclosed track which reaches Lenham Chest Hospital and the road beyond.

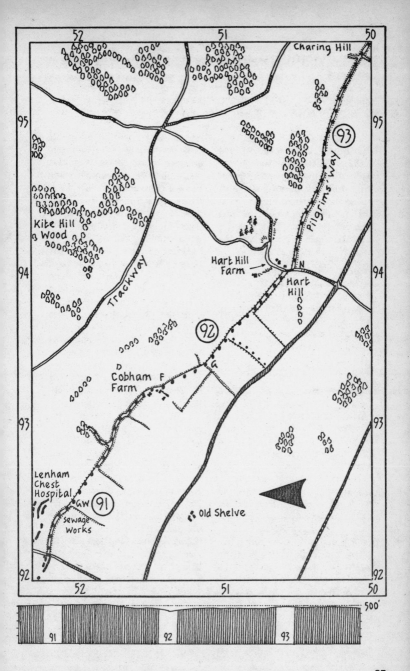

35. Charing, Burnthouse Farm, Stubyers Wood

2 miles
Maps: 1:25000 sheet TQ94; 1:50000 sheet 189

East-bound: On reaching the A252 cross over at an angle and walk down the metalled Pilgrims' Way. Just past Burnthouse Farm, on the approach to the quarry, bear left and then turn right to pass between the quarry buildings and some cottages. From then on the route is clear as far as the road.

West-bound: Where the metalling ceases continue forward to follow the clearly defined path along the edge of the wood to come out at a quarry. Continue forward past Burnthouse Farm along a metalled lane to reach the A252. Cross this at an angle and follow the metalled Pilgrims' Way.

Charing has a grocer's shop (early closing Tuesday), a post office, a bank, two public houses, the Royal Oak and the Queen's Head, and buses to Canterbury, Chartham, Old Wives Lees, Chilham, Ashford, Lenham, Harrietsham, Hollingbourne and Maidstone and train services to Ashford, Lenham, Harrietsham, Hollingbourne, Maidstone, Kemsing and London Victoria.

Charing is a most attractive village just off the path and is well worth visiting. It contains a considerable number of beautiful timber-framed houses and some attractive buildings delightfully grouped round the church. This was built in the thirteenth century but was damaged by a fire in 1590 caused by a Spaniard who managed to set fire to the roof by discharging his fowling-piece at it. It contains some interesting bench ends depicting Jack in the Green, a symbol of the pagan spirit of nature, a vamping-horn which was used to provide a loud humming noise to accompany the orchestra and some superb painted timbers in the roof. It once had a spurious relic which was supposed to be the block on which John the Baptist laid his head to be executed. This was probably destroyed in the fire. On the left, facing the church, is the Archbishop's Palace. Originally this was a manor house in which the bishops lived from the fourteenth century onwards, but it was enlarged on several occasions and Henry VIII stayed here on his way to the Field of Cloth of Gold. On the north side of the church is a large stone-built barn which was the banqueting hall of the Archbishop's Palace where Henry VIII was entertained. The church hall dates from the seventeenth century but was moved from High Halden in 1958.

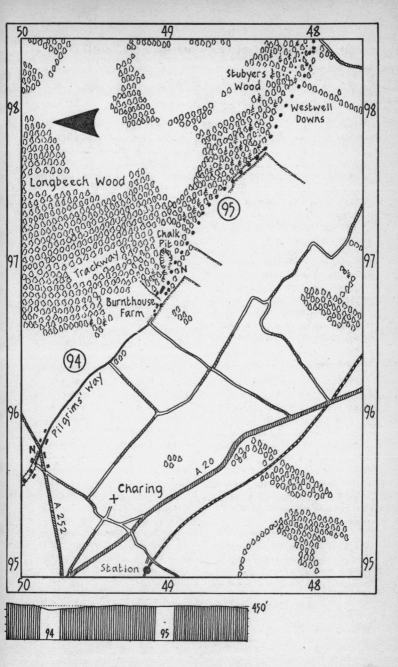

36. Dunn Street, Eastwell, Eastwell Park

$2\frac{1}{4}$ miles
Maps: 1:25000 sheets TQ94 and TR04; 1:50000 sheet 189

East-bound: Continue forward from Stubyers Wood to reach a road, turn left along a road and walk into the hamlet of Dunn Street. At the T-junction turn left and, about 50 yds later, turn right to follow a clear farm track through Eastwell Park. About 1 mile after leaving Dunn Street, turn right down a conifer wood and at the edge turn left and continue forward across a large field, making for the church which stands beside Eastwell Lake. Continue forward along the road, taking the left-hand fork by the church to reach a T-junction. At the T-junction cross over into the field and go straight on to reach a road, cross over, bear very slightly left and continue forward.

West-bound: On reaching the road at mile 98 cross over and enter the field, moving slightly away from the road on your right. *Do not cross the fence on your left.* On reaching the road continue forward to Eastwell church and the lake. Cross the road near the road junction and take the path that goes across the large field, aiming for the edge of a conifer plantation ahead. Continue past the conifer plantation, turn right along its far edge to meet a farm road, turn left and follow it all the way to the hamlet of Dunn Street.

On reaching the road turn left and almost immediately turn right to go down another road. Look for the path which goes off right about 200 yds after the first turning on the right.

Westwell, just off the path, has a post office stores (closed Monday afternoon and all day Wednesday), and a public house. The fine Early English parish church dates mainly from the thirteenth century. It has a vaulted chancel with a triple chancel arch and some beautifully carved stone choir stalls. The east window contains some thirteenth-century glass and depicts the Tree of Jesse. The lower two panels were made in 1960. Richard Barham, who wrote the *Ingoldsby Legends,* was curate here from 1814 to 1817 and there is a memorial in the church to his infant son Henry.

The fifteenth-century Eastwell church, severely damaged during the war, is in a beautiful setting beside the lake. The most interesting monuments were removed to the Victoria and Albert Museum and those interior furnishings which could be saved were found new homes in other churches. The church was said to contain the grave of Richard Plantagenet, the bastard son of Richard III.

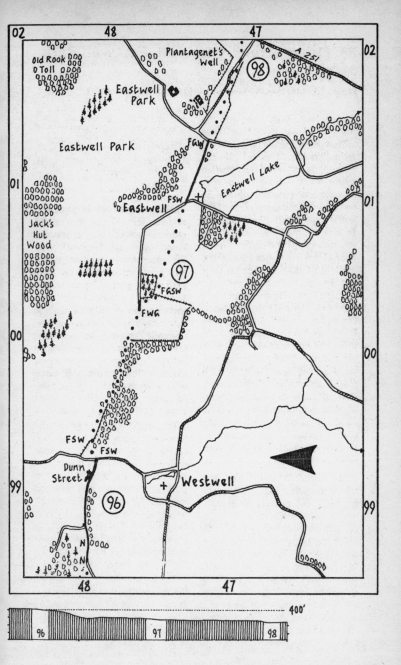

37. Boughton Lees, Wye

3 miles
Maps: 1:25000 sheet TR04; 1:50000 sheet 189

East-bound: Turn right off the main road at Boughton Lees village green. On the far side of the green, continue forward over the crossroads following the metalled Pilgrims' Way. About 200 yds after passing a lane on the left will be seen the Canterbury section of the Path signposted (see below). Follow the road for another 200 yds to where it bends to the left near a farm. Turn right here off the road and follow a fence on your left. The path turns left with the fence for 100 yds and then turns right to cross the field and reach the A28. Turn left along the road for a few yards and then turn right through an orchard, right and then immediately left to continue forward across several fields to a road. Turn left and follow the road, turn right over the level crossing and follow the main road into Wye. At the T-junction cross into the churchyard and follow a metalled path, keeping the church on your left, to meet a road.

West-bound: Cross the road and take a metalled path on the left between the college and allotments and pass through the churchyard to the road. Continue forward along the road opposite to the level crossing, turn left and, 100 yds later, right into a field. Cross several fields to arrive at the road near Perry Court Farm. Turn left for a few yards and then right across a field, turn left down a fence and then right, still following the fence, to a road. Turn left and follow the road all the way to the A251 at Boughton Lees.

Alternative Route (via Canterbury). Boughton Lees, Boughton Aluph
2 miles
East-bound: Turn right off the main road at the village green and, on the far side of the green, continue over the crossroads along the metalled Pilgrims' Way. 200 yds after passing a lane on the left, turn left along an enclosed path, then bear right to keep a hedge on your right and walk towards the road at Boughton Aluph church. Cross the road and continue to the far left-hand corner of the field to a complicated system of gates and pens. Continue forward downhill along an enclosed path and bear left round the back of a house to reach a road. (*Continue on p. 118.*)

West-bound: Cross the road and follow the path which bears left round a house, and is then enclosed with wire as it crosses a dip. On reaching a fence, turn left through some gates and pens and immediately right to continue forward to the road. Cross into the field next to the churchyard and continue forward to a road, turn right and follow the road to the A251 at Boughton Lees.

The parish church of All Saints, Boughton Aluph, is most interesting. It has a thirteenth-century chancel and fourteenth-century nave lit by five splendid Perpendicular windows.

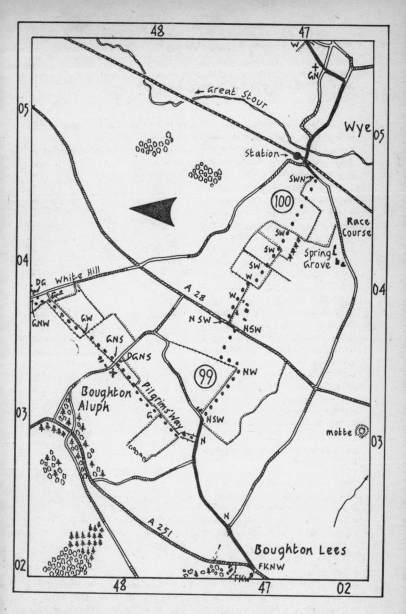

38. Wye, The Giant's Grave, Newgate Scrubs

2½ miles
Maps: 1:25000 sheet TR04; 1:50000 sheet 189

East-bound: Cross the road to a metalled lane which runs through the grounds of the Agricultural College. Where the metalling ceases continue forward through a large field, following the fence on your right. Cross the road and follow a fence on the left to the wood, continue through the wood until reaching the road, turn right and then 200 yds later turn right off the road and follow the path through wood and scrubland running parallel to the road. Follow the fence over Broad Downs through the National Nature Reserve, along the edge of Newgate Scrubs and into a field where the hedge on the left should be followed.

West-bound: Cross two stiles and walk along the edge of Newgate Scrubs. Ignore the significant track going off to the left downhill and continue along the fence running parallel to the road above you. After crossing Broad Downs the route is not clear through the wood, but if you bear round to the right you are bound to come to the road. Look for the metalled access road that joins the public road and walk down it for a few yards, then turn left through a gate into a field. Follow the fence on the right and then, near mile 102, bear round to the right to meet a road. Turn left, follow the road for 200 yds and turn off left through a path through the woods which drops steeply downhill towards a road. Cross a field and the road, continue forward with a fence on

your left-hand side and you will walk through the grounds of the Agricultural College to the road at Wye.

Wye has two grocer's shops, a post office, banks, two public houses and a café. Between them the two grocer's shops are open six full days each week. The official early closing day is Wednesday. There are bus services to Canterbury, Chartham, Chilham, Godmersham and Ashford and trains to Ashford, Chilham, Chartham, Canterbury, Ramsgate, London Charing Cross and London Victoria.

Wye is an attractive small town dominated by Wye College, the Agricultural School of London University, founded in 1892 as a successor to the college founded by Archbishop Kemp in the fifteenth century. It was he who rebuilt the parish church. In 1685 the tower fell, causing great damage to the east end. It was once believed that Wye was the birthplace of Mrs Aphra Behn, the noted seventeenth century feminist, novelist, playwright and spy, but Victoria Sackville-West demolished this legend.

The Wye and Gundale Downs National Nature Reserve was established as a good example of chalk downland and woodland and its characteristic flora and fauna. (Further information and leaflet from the Regional Officer, Nature Conservancy Council, Church Street, Wye, Ashford, Kent; tel. Wye 812525.)

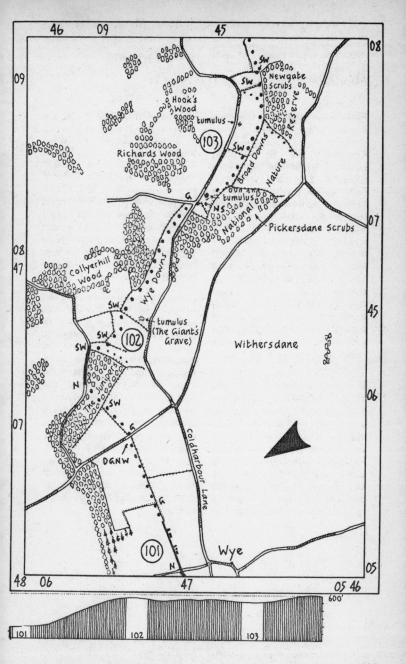

46 09   45   08

09   ᔕᗯ

                              ᔕᗯ   Newgate
                                        Scrubs
            Hook's
            Wood   tumulus   Reserve

                            103   Nature
            Richards Wood   ᔕᗯ

                                        Broad Downs

                              G   tumulus
                                  NS   National
                                                    ↑   Pickersdane Scrubs

08
47   Collyerhill
          Wood

                        Wye Downs
                ᔕᗯ
              ᔕᗯ   tumulus
            ᔕᗯ   102 (The Giant's
                        Grave)   Withersdane

07   N
              The Jumps
                    ᔕᗯ

                    G
                  DGNW
                            Coldharbour Lane

                    G
                101
                            Wye   05
48 06   47   05 46

600'

101   102   103

103

39. Cold Blow, Brabourne Downs, Brabourne

3 miles
Maps: 1:25000 sheets TR04 and TR14; 1:50000 sheet 189

East-bound: Cross the farm track and continue forward following a hedge on your right-hand side. Cross a stile and turn left to the road, turn right along the road and then left at the next road junction. Continue forward for $\frac{1}{4}$ mile and, where the road turns very sharply left, continue forward along a trackway which then runs along the edge of some fields to reach a road. At the road turn right and walk downhill, round a left hand bend and, where it turns slightly right, turn left through a gate along a hedge and into a wood where the path is enclosed by hedges.

West-bound: Follow the enclosed track to the end of the wood and then continue forward along the edge of the field to a road. Turn right, walk uphill and on the top you will see a wood on the left-hand side with a track running along the side of it. Turn left here and follow the track, which becomes enclosed and meets a road. At the road turn left and at the T-junction turn right. Follow this road for about 300 yds and then turn left over a stile. The path runs to the corner of the field and crosses a stile. The route is slightly complicated here, but you should be walking slightly away from the road on your right with a hedge on your left-hand side. Cross the farm track at Cold Blow, bear slightly left and go through a field.

Brabourne, just off the path, has a public house called the Five Bells. The church, a mixture of many styles, is very interesting. Much of it, including the chancel arch, is Norman work. The tower, too, is Norman and contains 30 steps cut from massive oak timbers. The east window is believed to be Norman and is probably the oldest complete glass window in England. There is an empty shrine which is believed once to have contained the heart of John Balliol, the founder of Balliol College, and there are some splendid brasses to the Scott family.

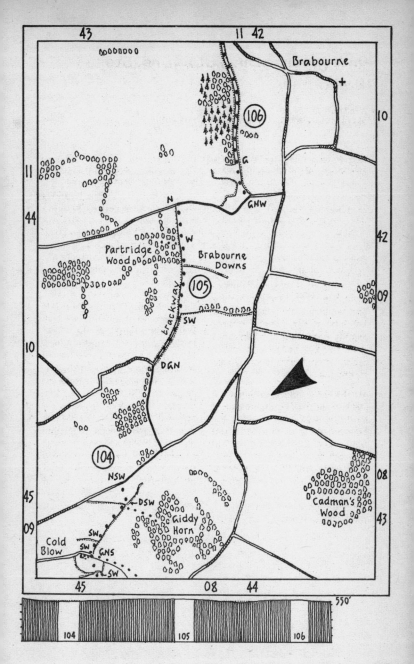

43   11 42

Brabourne

106

10

G

N

GNW

11

44

W

Partridge
Wood

Brabourne
Downs

105

trackway

SW

10

DGN

104

NSW

45

DSW

09

SW

Giddy
Horn

SW GNS

Cold
Blow

SW

Cadman's
Wood

08

43

45   08   44

550'

| 104 | 105 | 106 |

40. Brabourne Lane, Stowting, Stone Street

3 miles
Maps: 1:25000 sheet T R14; 1:50000 sheet 189

East-bound: Cross Brabourne Lane, following the enclosed track which will bring you to a narrow lane, turn left and follow this, ignoring all roads that turn off, until, about 50 yds before a road junction, turn left up a narrow path, cross a road and continue forward up a hill following a fence. At the top of the hill, continue forward and then cross to the other side of the fence by a stile. On reaching the road, turn right, keeping inside the field edge, to a stile at a road. Continue forward still inside the field edge. Cross a number of stiles and about 200 yds after passing the picnic place and road junction on your left, turn left, cross the road and follow a track which meets the fence and then runs down it keeping it on your left.

West-bound: Where the fence turns a corner, continue forward to the road and then cross over and turn right along the field edge, walking parallel to the road, across a number of stiles until reaching a road junction. Cross over and continue walking parallel to the road until meeting a fence, turn left and follow the fence to the end of the field. Cross the fence by a stile and continue in the same direction on the other side to reach a road. Cross the road and continue forward down a narrow path to meet another road. Turn right and follow this road, ignoring roads that lead off, past the Anchor Inn and Stowting Court. Half a mile beyond the Anchor Inn look for a track which forks off right. Follow this to a road and then continue forward.

The parish church of Stowting has been 'restored out of existence' (*Buildings of England: North East and East Kent*), but there is some good fourteenth-century glass.

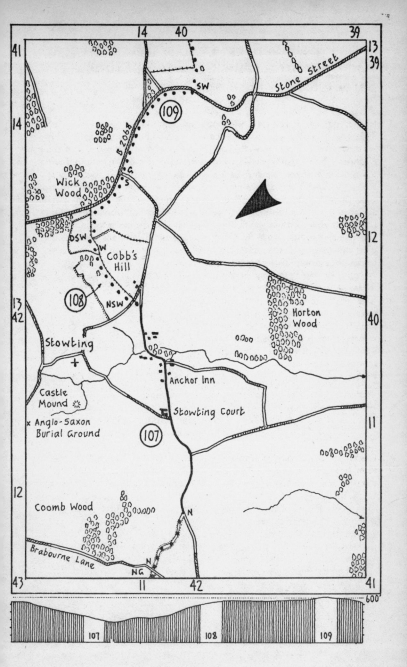

41. Postling, Staple Farm, Coombe Farm

3¼ miles
Maps: 1:25000 sheet TR13; 1:50000 sheet 189

East-bound: Follow a series of fences running parallel to, but above, the road and Postling church. Near Postling Wood turn right, walk towards the road and then turn left, inside the field edge, to meet the road at a road junction. Cross over the road and walk up the left-hand side of the fence to a wireless station. Keep to the left of this, cross the access road and continue forward keeping a fence on your left. On reaching the wood, turn left and follow the edge of the wood to a road near Etchinghill Hospital. At the road turn right and almost immediately left down a farm road. 100 yds later turn left over a stile into a field.

West-bound: Walk to the top of the field to a stile and you will arrive at a farm road, turn right to the road at the top and then turn right again in a few yards, looking for a stile on the left which follows a wood. Walk alongside the wood to the fence at the top, cross it, turn right and walk to the wireless station. Keep to the right of the wireless station, cross the access road and, emerging on the other side, continue forward with the fence on your left to reach Staple Farm. Cross the road, enter the field and immediately turn left and follow the edge of the field, parallel to the road, to a fence. Turn right at the fence and then turn left through a gate following a fence running parallel to the road. Leave the fence and follow the line of the downs above Postling church and then continue forward keeping a fence on your right-hand side for most of the way.

The Pent was the home of Joseph Conrad from 1898 to 1907. While he lived here he wrote a number of novels, including *Lord Jim*, and was visited by such literary luminaries as George Bernard Shaw, H. G. Wells and Henry James.

Postling is an attractive hamlet but has no facilities. The church dates from the twelfth century and was built by the Premonstratensian Canons of St Radegund's Abbey and has the unusual dedication to St Mary and St Radegund. It is basically Norman. The chancel was extended in the fourteenth century. It has a fine fifteenth-century roof and there are traces of wall paintings in the nave.

Etchinghill, just off the Path, has a public house, the New Inn, and a café. There are bus services to Canterbury and Folkestone.

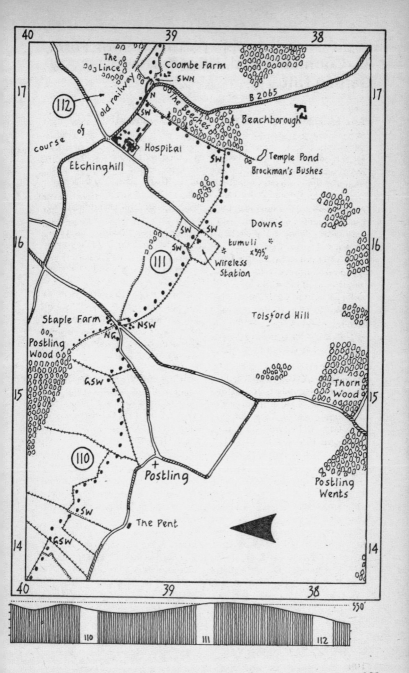

40   39   38

The Lince

Coombe Farm

SWN

112

course of old railway

N

The Beeches

B 2065

Beachborough

SW

SW

Hospital

Temple Pond

Brockman's Bushes

Etchinghill

Downs

SW   SW

SW

111

tumuli

x395

Wireless Station

Tolsford Hill

Staple Farm

NSW

NG

Postling Wood

GSW

Thorn Wood

110

Postling

Postling Wents

SW

The Pent

GSW

550'

110   111   112

42. Coombe Wood, Hungar Down, Cherry Garden Hill

3 miles
Maps: 1:25000 sheets T R13 and T R23; 1:50000 sheet 189

East-bound: Make your way through the fields to Coombe Wood and then turn left under the railway arch. Continue forward over a stile and climb steeply uphill to meet a fence. Turn right and, keeping this fence on your left, follow it all the way to an enclosed track. Turn right along this track to the road at Hungar Down. (At the time of writing the route through the field is not open and it is necessary to keep to the road all the way to Cherry Garden Hill.)

West-bound: Follow the road from Cherry Garden Hill, noting that at the second road junction the route across the fields has not yet been negotiated and it is necessary to keep to the road as far as Hungar Down. Look for an enclosed track that runs off to the left about 100 yds beyond the entrance to the house. Follow this track for about $\frac{1}{4}$ mile and then turn off left across a stile. The whole of this section has fierce notices warning walkers that this is an army training area. After leaving the enclosed track continue to a gate and a stile and then on to another stile. A couple of hundred yards beyond this stile look for a gully which goes off to the left steeply downhill near a junction of tracks. Follow this and you will arrive at the railway arch. Pass underneath and almost immediately turn right and walk through the wood.

Paddlesworth has a public house with the unusual name of the Cat and Custard Pot. The parish church of St Oswald is a tiny Norman building only 48 ft long and 20 ft wide.

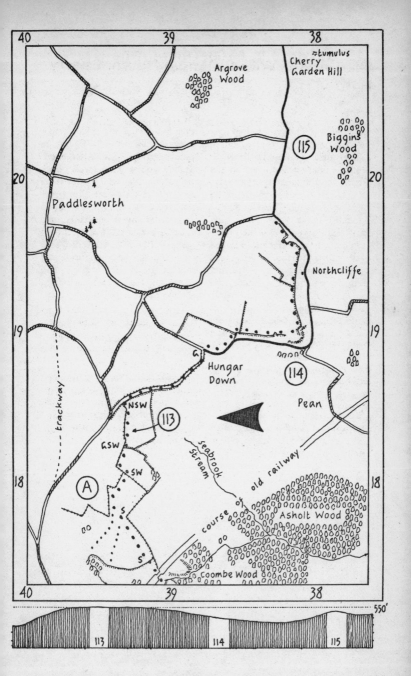

43. Castle Hill, A260, Dover Hill

2 miles
Maps: 1:25000 sheet T R23; 1:50000 sheet 189

East-bound: Follow the road past the kennels to a road junction. Turn right and follow a path which runs parallel to the road on the right-hand side of the field and then bears left through the motte and bailey castle. The path almost doubles back on itself, just touches the road, and then continues, with splendid views across Folkestone, to the A260. Cross this road and continue forward along a metalled lane. After about 200 yds it is possible to walk inside the field edge on the right-hand side though, in places, thoughtless motorists have used it as a rubbish dump. On reaching the main road at Dover Hill walk down the right-hand side of the Valiant Sailor public house and then turn left.

West-bound: Turn right away from the cliffs and walk to the main road at the Valiant Sailor public house. Cross over into Crete Road East and almost immediately turn left and walk inside the field edge parallel to the road. After about $\frac{3}{4}$ mile you will be forced back on to the road which should be followed to the A260. Cross over and immediately turn left over a stile to follow a path that runs roughly parallel to the road, then sweeps round the edge of Castle Hill, doubles back on itself and rejoins the road. Turn left and follow the road which runs along the top of the downs.

Folkestone Castle, now little more than earthworks, was a Norman motte and bailey castle. When excavated, traces of wall were found and a well sunk to a depth of 84 ft in order to strike water in the chalk. There is a record of a Priory Church near the castle but this probably refers to another bailey on the east side of the parish church.

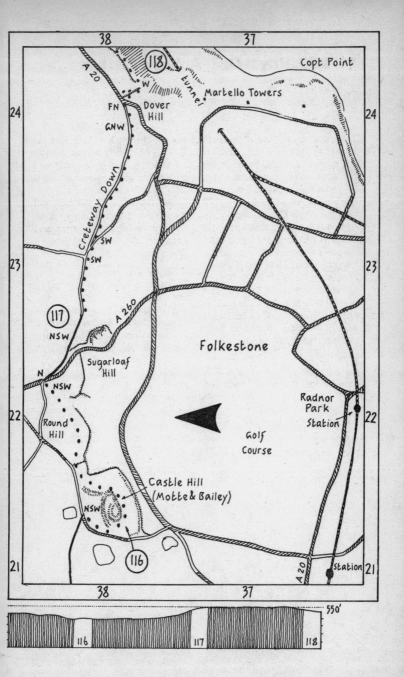

44. A20, Royal Oak, Abbot's Cliff

2½ miles
Maps: 1:25000 sheet T R23; 1:50000 sheet 189

East-bound: Follow the path along the top of the cliff, which is sometimes squeezed between the cliff edge and caravan sites and at others runs almost touching the road, until forced onto the A20 near the Royal Oak public house. At this point a decision has to be made. If red flags are flying from the cliffs above Lydden Spout the firing range is in use and it will be necessary to follow the path which runs inside the field edge on the right-hand side of the A20. If no red flag is flying then bear right along the enclosed track and climb to the top of the cliffs.

West-bound: Main route: Follow the path along the fence which then drops down an enclosed track and joins the A20 near the Royal Oak public house. Almost immediately, turn left and follow a path round some houses which is later sometimes squeezed between the edge of the cliff and road or a caravan site. After 1 mile, the path swings to the right and joins the A20 near the Valiant Sailor public house.

Alternative route:
Those who have been forced to use the alternative route because the Lydden Spout firing range was in use should follow the path inside the field edge, just to the left of the A20, to near the Royal Oak public house. From now on follow the route description above.

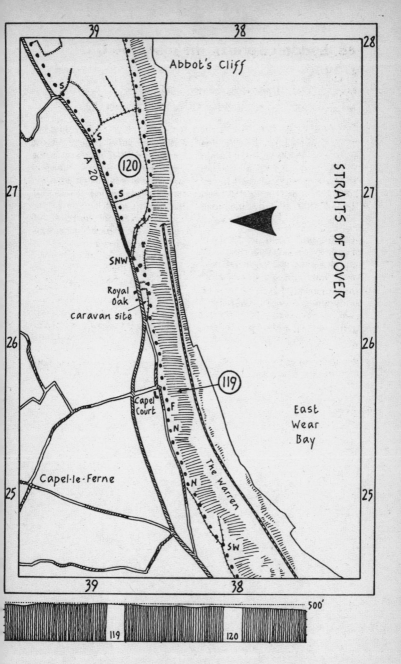

Abbot's Cliff

STRAITS OF DOVER

A 20

120

S

S

S

SNW

Royal
Oak

caravan site

119

East
Wear
Bay

Capel
Court

F

N

Capel·le·Ferne

The Warren

N

SW

500'

119   120

45. Lydden Spout, Shakespeare Cliff, Dover

$2\frac{1}{2}$ miles
Maps: 1:25000 sheets TR23 and TR34; 1:50000 sheet 189

East-bound: Follow the cliff edge past the Lydden Spout firing range, then continue forward until, after a mile and a half, forced on to the road beyond Shakespeare Cliff. Follow the road downhill all the way into Dover.

West-bound: From the centre of Dover follow Shargate Road past the Hoverport and Western Docks and fork right along Archcliffe Road. Ahead of you will be seen the enormous bulk of Shakespeare Cliff. Where the road bears sharply right, turn left and keep to the cliff edge climbing steeply upwards. Follow the cliff all the way past the Lydden Spout firing range. If the Lydden Spout firing range is in use, which is indicated by a red flag flying, turn right past the range building to meet a road. At the road turn right again and after 200 yds turn left through a gateway and continue forward over some stiles steeply downhill to the main A20 road. At the A20 road turn left inside the field edge adjacent to the main road.

For a description of Dover see p. 145. There is a map of the town on p. 141.

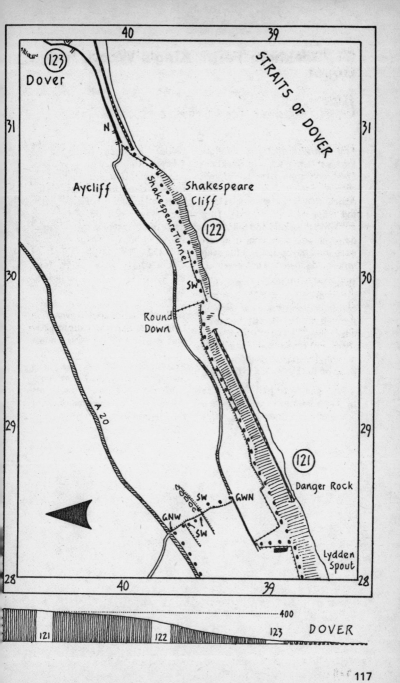

Dover

123

Aycliff

Shakespeare Tunnel

Shakespeare Cliff

STRAITS OF DOVER

N

122

SW

Round Down

A 20

121

Danger Rock

SW GWN

GNW

SW

Lydden Spout

400

121 122 123 DOVER

C1. Soakham Farm, King's Wood, Ridge Wood

3 miles

Maps: 1:25000 sheets TR04 and TR05/15; 1:50000 sheet 179

East-bound: From the road follow the clear farm track past Soakham Farm and then bear left uphill, keeping a fence on your left. Bear right and then turn sharp left along the edge of some woods. Turn right into the wood and follow the path through a number of clearings. Just beyond mile 3 the path runs inside the edge of the wood.

West-bound: Follow the path just inside the edge of the wood and continue along the clear track to turn left on the edge of the wood near mile 2. The path then turns sharp right and then bears left downhill to pass Soakham Farm. Keep on the clear track to the road.

This section of path runs close to Godmersham Park and the house may be seen in the valley below. It once belonged to Edward Knight, who was Jane Austen's brother and changed his name by deed poll to please his in-laws and to secure his inheritance. Jane was very fond of him and came often to stay in this beautiful Palladian house, which was built in 1732. The parish church of Godmersham dates mainly from the Norman period with some later additions. It contains a bas-relief of Thomas à Becket on the south wall of the chancel, which is believed to date from about 1200 and may well be the oldest representation of the Archbishop extant. The east window is a memorial to Edward Knight, who died in 1852, and there are monuments to earlier members of the Knight family.

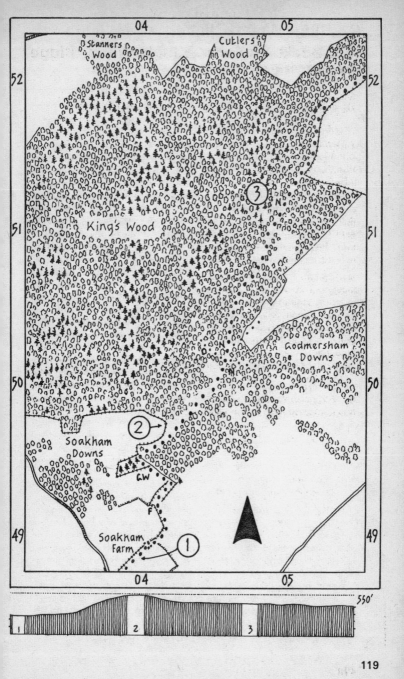

C2. Ridge Wood, Chilham, Old Wives Lees

3 miles
Maps: 1:25000 sheet TR05/15; 1:50000 sheet 179

East-bound: After leaving Ridge Wood the path goes downhill between fences, then takes a sharp left-hand bend and reaches a road. Continue forward down the road to Chilham. Turn right by the pub and walk down the left-hand side of the churchyard to meet the road again. Continue forward across the main road and then the minor road to reach Old Wives Lees. Go over the crossroads, keeping to the road.

West-bound: Go over the crossroads at Old Wives Lees and follow the lane to another crossroads and then forward to the A252. Continue forward towards Chilham and, on the left-hand side of the lane, there is an inconspicuous path that runs up through the churchyard to the centre of Chilham. On emerging in the square, take the lane that runs off to the left past the post office. After a mile it takes a sharp left-hand turn. At this point leave it and continue forward along a clearly defined path which shortly turns right and then climbs uphill between fences into Ridge Wood.

Chilham has a grocer's shop, a post office, a public house, the White Horse, a restaurant, buses to Ashford and Canterbury and trains to Wye, Ashford, London Victoria and London Charing Cross, Chartham and Canterbury.

Chilham is as pretty as a picture postcard. Chilham Castle is a Jacobean house built in 1616 by Sir Dudley Digges. In the grounds are the remains of the old Norman castle keep, itself built on the site of the Saxon hall. The church dates mainly from the fifteenth century. During the Reformation the shrine of St Augustine of Canterbury was dismantled and brought to the church to escape the malevolent hands of the reformers. However, Thomas Cranmer insisted that it be removed and it was probably broken up. In 1860, during restoration, a large empty Purbeck marble sarcophagus was discovered, but there is no proof that it was ever St Augustine's tomb. The church contains some fine monuments and a charming sculpture of two boys who died in 1858. They are shown with a battledore and shuttlecock at their feet and with a book, *Babes in the Wood*.

The neolithic long barrow on Julliberrie Downs, near the railway, was once thought to be the grave of a Roman Tribune, Julius Laberius, but when it was opened in the 1930s, although four Roman burials were found, none was of a Tribune and they were graves of people who had died about a century later than Julius.

Old Wives Lees has a post office stores, early closing Wednesday, which lies beside the route, and a public house, the Star. It is an unattractive place and the only remarkable thing is its name, which is probably a corruption of Oldwood's Lees, meaning 'clearings in a wood'.

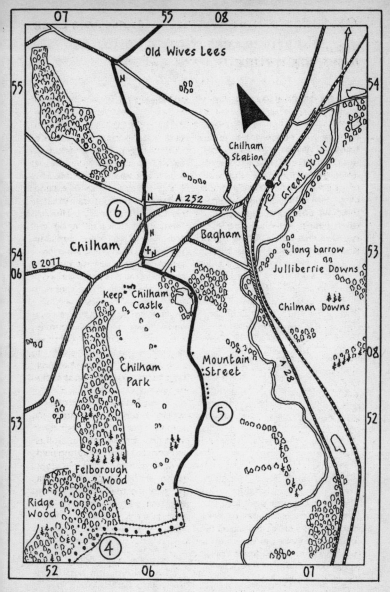

07　55　08

Old Wives Lees

55　54

Chilham Station

Great Stour

　Chilham Station

N　A 252

⑥

N

Bagham

Chilham

N

54　06

B 2077

long barrow

Julliberrie Downs

Chilman Downs

Keep Chilham Castle

N

Mountain Street

53　52

A 28

⑤

Chilham Park

Felborough Wood

Ridge Wood

④

52　06　07

400'

4　5　6

C3. Old Wives Lees, Nickle Farm, Chartham Hatch

2¾ miles

Maps: 1:25000 sheet TR05/15; 1:50000 sheet 179

East-bound: Follow the road out of Old Wives Lees to a road junction. Fork left and, a few yards later, cross the road and walk down a path enclosed by fences and trees. On reaching a broad track which crosses, turn right and then almost immediately left, to walk steeply uphill. At the top of the hill the path turns sharply left and then turns right over a stile, down the edge of a wood, past a shack in an orchard and on to the railway. Cross the railway by the level crossing, turn right and follow the road. On reaching a road junction at Nickle Farm, continue forward along a path which runs uphill beside some trees to meet a road, turn left and follow the road, forking right along a track just beyond a house. The path runs behind the back of what appears to be a small factory to emerge at the road, turn left and then almost immediately right following the road past the Chapter Arms Inn to a T-junction, turn left and then turn right down the narrowed metalled footpath which runs beside the grocer's shop. On reaching a road cross over and follow the path into a wood past a children's playground.

West-bound: On reaching a road by the children's playground cross over and take the narrow metalled path to the road in the centre of Chartham Hatch. Turn left, then almost immediately right and follow the narrow road past the Chapter Arms Inn to a T-junction. Turn left and almost immediately right round the back of a factory, following a clear track which will bring you to a metalled farm road. Follow this road along the edge of Fright Wood, and where it turns sharply left at the edge of the wood near some poplar trees, turn right down a narrow steep path to Nickle Farm. At the road cross over and follow the farm road, turning off it left at the railway. Cross the railway by the level crossing and take the track that heads uphill, past a shed, to a stile on the edge of a wood. Cross the stile, turn left and then follow the field edge to where it turns right and drops steeply downhill to a farm track. Turn right for a few yards and then left uphill through some hop fields to reach a stile which gives access to an enclosed path. Follow this path to the road, take the road opposite and, a few yards later, bear right and walk into Old Wives Lees.

Chartham Hatch has a post office stores and a public house, the Chapter Arms Inn, both beside the route. Early closing day is Wednesday.

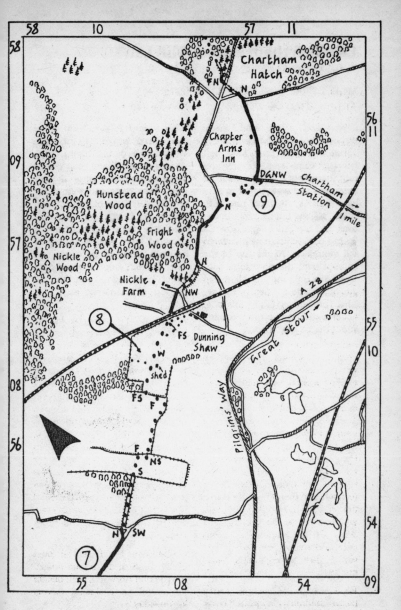

C4. Chartham Hatch, Mill Lane

2 miles
Maps: 1:25000 sheet T R05/15; 1:50000 sheet 179

East-bound: The path runs through the wood, bears right and about 300 yds later forks left between some trees. 150 yds later turn sharp right to meet a metalled farm lane and walk uphill to a T-junction. At the road turn left, cross the new bridge over the by-pass and then turn right down a fenced path which runs parallel to the motorway. At the top of the embankment the path turns left, drops downhill and then climbs up the other side to meet a narrow lane. Turn left and follow this lane, which will bring you to a round-about on the next map.

West-bound: Where the metalled lane goes downhill, look for a path which strikes off to the right, drops steeply downhill and then climbs up to an embankment on the by-pass. Turn right and follow the fenced path to the bridge, turn left across the bridge and then immediately turn right down a metalled farm lane. A couple of hundred yards or so down the lane, fork left along a broad path which will bring you to the outskirts of Chartham Hatch.

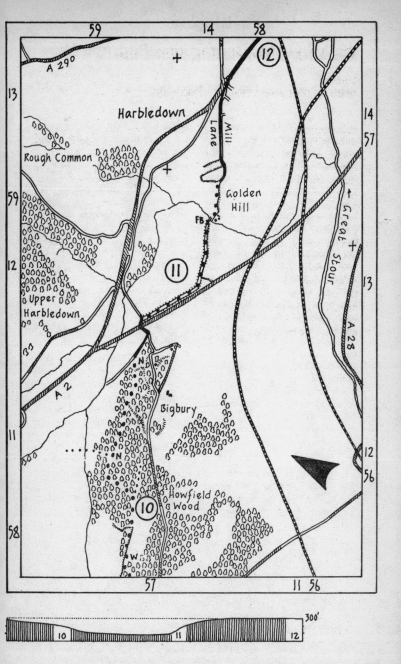

Harbledown

Rough Common

Golden Hill

FB

Upper Harbledown

Bigbury

Howfield Wood

Mill Lane

A 290

Great Stour

A 28

A 2

⑩ ⑪ ⑫

13
14
57
59
12
11
58
14
13
12
56
11 56
57
59 14 58

300'
10   11   12

125

C5. Mill Lane, Canterbury, Pilgrims' Way

3 miles
Maps: 1:25000 sheet TR05/15; 1:50000 sheet 179

East-bound: Continue down Mill Lane until reaching the roundabout. Cross over, aiming for the prominent church, and follow the pavement which runs alongside the recreation ground. Cross to the other side of the road by the subway near the public conveniences and continue in the same direction until reaching the next roundabout. Turn left here and walk along St Peter's Place to the traffic lights by the city gate. Turn right and walk through the pedestrian precinct of Long Market. At the roundabout continue forward under the subway along St George's Place. At the next traffic lights turn left along Lower Chantry Lane, turn right down Spring Lane and then turn right again down Pilgrims' Way. Turn left along St Augustine's Road and Pilgrims' Way, turn right and cross the railway along Pilgrims' Lane, which leaves the city and makes for Patrixbourne.

West-bound: Follow the metalled lane until reaching the railway bridge, turn left along Pilgrims' Way and then right down St Augustine's Road. On reaching the T-junction at the church turn left and follow the main road, which is called Lower Chantry Lane, to the traffic lights. Turn right and then continue forward under the subway to Long Market, which is a pedestrian precinct. At the traffic lights by the city gate turn left and walk to the roundabout. Turn right at the roundabout and make for the roundabout ahead. After a short distance cross the road by the subway and then continue in the same direction to the roundabout. At the roundabout bear off left along Mill Lane.

Canterbury has a population of 36,000 with bus services to most parts of east Kent and trains to Aylesham, Dover, Chartham, Chilham, Wye, Ashford, Charing, Lenham, Harrietsham, Hollingbourne, Maidstone, London Victoria and London Charing Cross. There is an information centre in St Peter's Street (tel. Canterbury 66567). Early closing day is Thursday. (*For a description of Canterbury see p. 144.*)

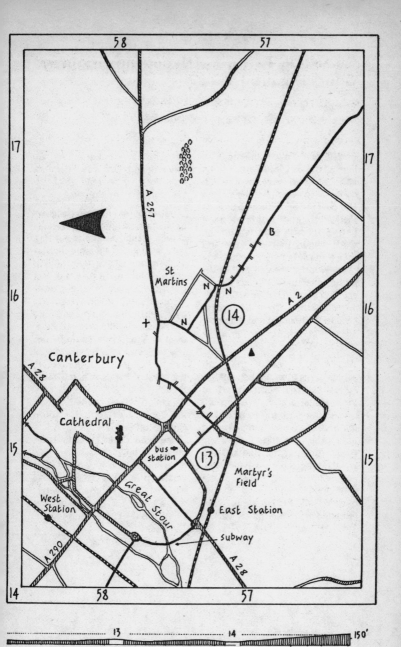

58   57

17   17

A 257

B

St Martins

N N

+ N

A 2

16   (14)   16

Canterbury

Cathedral

bus station

(13)

Martyr's Field

15   15

A 28

West Station

Great Stour

East Station

A 290

subway

A 28

14   58   57

13 .... 14 .... 150'

C6. Hode Farm, Patrixbourne, Highland Court Hospital

2½ miles
Maps: 1:25000 sheet TR05/15; 1:50000 sheet 179

East-bound: Follow the metalled lane all the way into Patrixbourne and, at the mini-roundabout, continue forward past the church and over the bridge which crosses the Nail Bourne. Just beyond the bridge the path turns left off the road, follows the field edge and then turns right to follow the edge of the wood all the way to the new bridge over the by-pass. *On no account cross the waymarked stile into the wood*. Cross the access road to the hospital and then bear left across a field, moving away from the A2.

West-bound: Follow the path across the field to the edge of the A2. Cross the access road to the hospital and walk alongside the A2 until coming to a field at the edge of a wood. Turn right and follow the field edge around the wood, ignoring the stile and the waymark on the right-hand side. Follow the edge of the field all the way down to the road on the outskirts of Patrixbourne. Turn right and walk through the village

to the mini-roundabout. Continue forward and 200 yds later fork right along a minor road which will take you into Canterbury.

Patrixbourne has no facilities but has a most interesting Norman church, dating from about 1160, with a magnificent south doorway. It contains a lot of good glass, including 18 panels dating from the sixteenth and seventeenth century which were made by Swiss craftsmen and are believed to be the work of Peter Bock of Altdorf and Martin Moser. The subjects in the Bifrons chapel include a pilgrimage to Jerusalem, the story of Pyramus and Thisbe, the Raising of Lazarus, the Adoration of the Shepherds, John the Baptist by the Jordan and a Crucifixion Scene.

Highland Court Hospital is an attractive building which looks much older than it actually is. It was built in 1904 for the racing motorist Count Zabrowski, who is remembered for his famous car Chitty-Chitty-Bang-Bang.

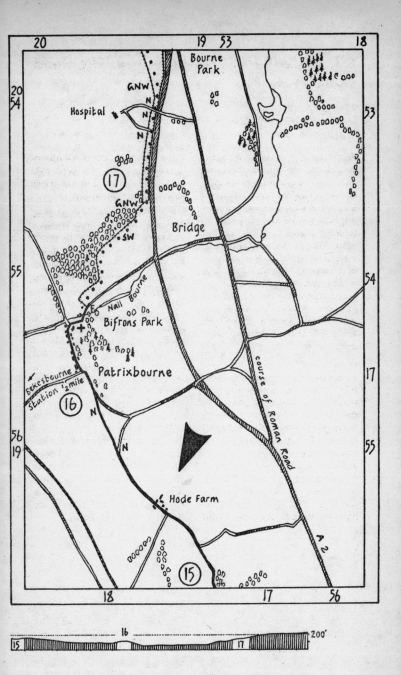

C7. Barham Downs, Upper Digges Place

2½ miles
Maps: 1:25000 sheets TR05/15 and TR25; 1:50000 sheet 179

East-bound: Cross the road and continue forward, keeping the fence on your left. Where the fence turns sharp left continue forward for nearly half a mile to reach another road. Cross over and go straight on across a fence to a road. Cross over and continue forward past a waymarked pole to reach a fence. Follow the fence to Upper Digges Place, cross the farm road and make for the enclosed track ahead which runs down the side of a cemetery.

West-bound: Follow the enclosed path to the road at Upper Digges Place. Pass the farm building, then almost immediately turn right off the farm road to follow a fence on your right-hand side. Where the fence bears sharp right to run up towards a wood, continue forward to reach a road. Cross the road and continue forward across a fence to reach another road. Go straight on across a very long field, which if you have negotiated properly will bring you alongside a field edge to a road. Cross the road and continue along the field edge.

Many of the fields in this section of the route are likely to be ploughed and sometimes it may be difficult to follow the exact line of the path.

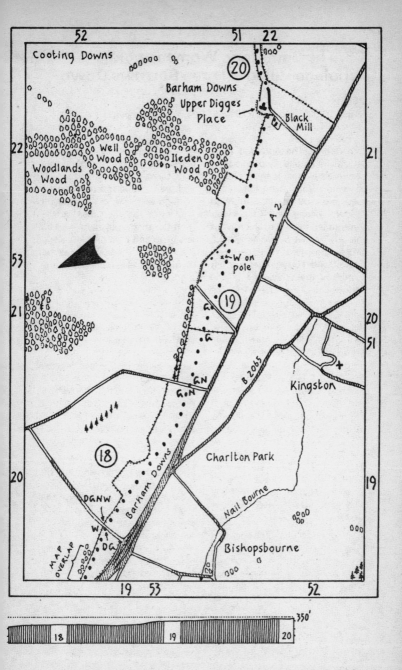

Cooting Downs

Barham Downs
Upper Digges
Place

Black
Mill

A 2

Well
Wood

Ileden
Wood

Woodlands
Wood

x x W on
pole

20

19

G

G

B 2065

Kingston

G N

G N

18

Charlton Park

Barham Downs

Nail Bourne

DGNW

W

DG

MAP
OVERLAP

Bishopsbourne

350'

18   19   20

131

C8. The Cemetery, Womenswold, Woolage Village, Three Barrows Down

2½ miles
Maps: 1:25000 sheets TR25 and TR24; 1:50000 sheet 179

East-bound: The enclosed track opens out into a field and then continues alongside the cemetery to reach a road. Turn left at the road and, 100 yds later, right to follow a hedge which takes you through a farmyard to the road in the tiny hamlet of Womenswold. Cross the road and continue forward and, 100 yds later, turn left to follow the other side of the hedge. Cross a couple of fences keeping the hedge on your right until arriving at the road. Cross the road, taking a narrow path through the little wood to meet the road on the other side, turn right and walk almost to the cross-roads. Just before reaching the crossroads, turn left across a stile and walk down the field edge to the recreation ground. Half way down the recreation ground cross the stile and walk to the road. At the road, turn left and continue forward until it bears sharply left. At this point continue forward along an enclosed track which will take you over Three Barrows Down.

West-bound: Follow the enclosed track to meet the road and continue forward for three or four hundred yards. Ignore a road which forks off to the left but almost immediately turn right across the recreation ground to a stile. Cross the stile, then turn left and walk to the top of the field, keeping as close to the road on your left as possible. Cross the stile onto the road, turn right for 100 yds or so and then turn left along a narrow path through the wood to meet another road. Cross the road and walk down the field, keeping the hedge on your left-hand side through a couple of fences. Near the outskirts of Womenswold cross to the other side of the hedge and then continue in the same direction until reaching the road in the hamlet. Cross over and walk through the farmyard, following a hedge on your right, until coming to the B2046. Turn left and 100 yds later turn right down a track which runs beside the cemetery.

Womenswold has no facilities and has the air of being cut off from the outside world. The parish church dates mainly from the thirteenth century and has some attractive eighteenth-century wall monuments.

Woolage has a post office stores at the crossroads beside the path. It is closed on Wednesday and Saturday afternoons.

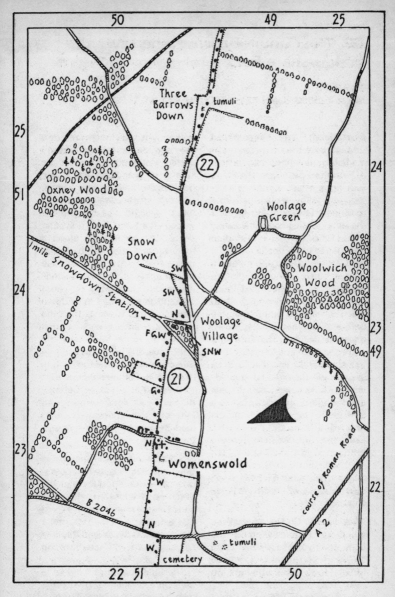

50 49 25

Three
Barrows
Down
tumuli

25

22

24

Oxney Wood
51

Woolage
Green

Snow
Down
SW

24
SW
N
Woolage
Village
FGW
SNW

Woolwich
Wood

23
49

21

G.

G.

N
Womenswold

W

23
22

B 2046

course of Roman Road

N

A 2

W
cemetery
tumuli

22 51
50

350'

21
22

C9. West Court Downs, Sibertswold, Waldershare Park

3 miles
Maps: 1:25000 sheet TR24; 1:50000 sheet 179

East-bound: On reaching the road turn left over the railway and immediately turn right (signposted to Eythorne) past Longlane Farm, turn right beside Longlane Cottage and follow a clear path to a road near a level crossing. Go over the level crossing and immediately turn left down a narrow path which goes diagonally across a field, crosses a road and follows a private road for a short distance to reach a playing field. Go diagonally across the playing field to reach a metalled path, cross the path and continue forward down a road to the main road. Turn right and almost immediately left beside the churchyard and into a field. Walk down the right-hand headland to a line of trees, cross the stile and then turn diagonally left to a stile in the far corner. Continue forward crossing the old railway. Cross into another field to arrive at the road near the church, turn right, walk to the crossroads, turn diagonally left along a path which runs besides a wood, cross a fence and continue to a wood.

West-bound: On the edge of the wood go diagonally across the park, aiming for the left-hand side of the wood ahead. Continue forward to the road, turn right, go over the crossroads past the church, and turn left along a path which skirts the church, crosses a field and the old railway to reach a stile. Continue forward at the stile to go diagonally across the field to the line of trees ahead. Cross the stile and walk up the left-hand headland past the churchyard to the road. Turn right and almost immediately left along a road, cross a metalled path and over a stile. Follow the field edge on the right and then go diagonally across the playing field to a stile and gate at a road. Walk down the road and bear left to go diagonally across some rough pasture to reach the road. Turn right, cross the level crossing and turn off left just before the left fork in the road. Follow the clear path to the road at Longlane Cottage, turn left, walk along the road, turn left across the railway and immediately turn right to follow a track.

Sibertswold, also known as Sheperdswell, has two grocer's, one closed on Monday and the other on Wednesday afternoon and Saturday afternoon, a post office, three public houses, and a bus service to Dover and trains to Dover, Aylesham, Canterbury and London Victoria.

The little church at Coldred is built on a Roman earthwork and dates from the thirteenth century.

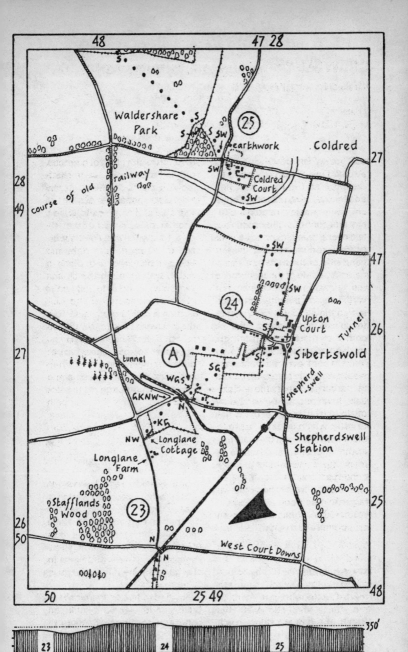

C10. Waldershare Park, Minacre Farm, Cane Wood

3 miles
Maps: 1:25000 sheets TR24 and TR34; 1:50000 sheet 179

East-bound: From the edge of the wood walk diagonally across the park to where a driveway and the road meet. Turn left along the driveway to the road, turn right and follow the road past the house and round the left-hand bend to a crossroads. At the crossroads turn left over a stile aiming for a circle of trees and walk round the left-hand side of the trees to a kissing gate and a stile at the far corner of the field. Go through the churchyard, keeping the church on your left, to the A256. Cross over, walk to the stile in the bottom left-hand corner of the field, turn left and follow the field boundary to the fence. Cross over the fence and walk diagonally across the field to the far corner. Ignore the enclosed track and continue forward, diagonally, to the far corner of the field to a stile which gives access to the road. Turn left along the road, right at the T-junction and, where the road turns very sharply left, continue forward along an enclosed track which then crosses a large field and continues on to a road. Turn right, go over the crossroads and 100 yds later look for an enclosed track which runs off to the left.

West-bound: Follow the enclosed track past Cane Wood to meet the road. Continue forward over the crossroads and, about 200 yds later, turn left over a stile and walk to the stile ahead. Cross the stile, continue forward across a large field and enter an enclosed track which meets the road. Follow the road forward, at the road junction turn left and, about 300 yds later, look for a stile on the right-hand side. Go diagonally across the field to a gate and continue forward to another gate. Pass through this gate, follow the edge of the wood and then turn right into the next field and on to the road. Cross the A256, walk through the churchyard to a kissing gate and aim for the bottom corner of the field, skirting a clump of trees. Go over the crossroads and follow the road round past Waldershare House. Just beyond the house, where a driveway meets the road, turn left and walk across the park, aiming for a stile on the edge of the wood.

Waldershare House was built at the beginning of the eighteenth century for Sir Henry Furnese, who also laid out the splendid park, parts of which are now under the plough. In 1913 the interior of the house was remodelled and it has recently been converted to luxury flats.

The little church of All Saints contains some monuments to the Monins family, including two colossal figures of Peregrine Bertie and his wife Susan, fourth daughter of Sir Edward Monins, who died in 1663. The tomb of Sir Henry Furnese, who built the house, is on the other side of the church and is a most ornate creation.

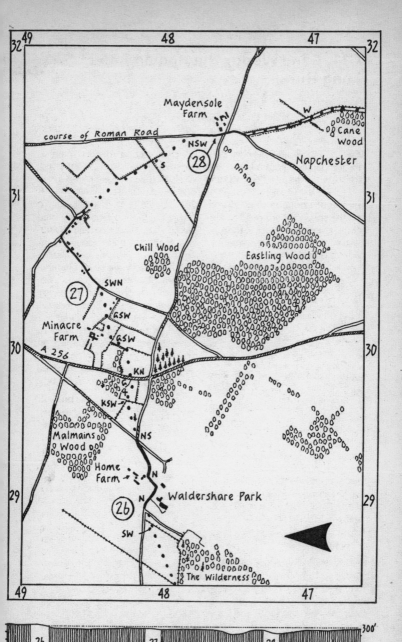

C11. Cane Wood, The Roman Road, Long Hill

2 miles
Maps: 1:25000 sheet TR34; 1:50000 sheet 179

East-bound: Follow the clear path to the road and continue forward for 100 yds or so until the track runs off to the left to reach the road at Pineham. Continue forward and, on the second sharp bend, go on along an enclosed track to the road at Sandwich Hole. Continue forward along the road.

West-bound: Where the metalling ceases at Sandwich Hole continue forward along an enclosed track to the road at Pineham. Where the road turns sharply left follow an enclosed track straight on to a road. Continue forward for 100 yds to where the road turns sharp right, leave the road and keep straight on along a clear track which heads for the wood.

This section of the path is following the line of the old Roman road from Richborough to Dover. At Church Whitfield, just off the path, is a small church which, although heavily restored in 1894, still contains much Saxon work and there are traces of wall paintings. For those who enjoy such things there is an eloquent commentary on the uncertainty of life in Victorian times in the gravestone of the Cross family in the churchyard. They had 12 children, of whom no less than 10 died within a fortnight of their birth, one lived for 15 months and only the twelfth lived on into adulthood.

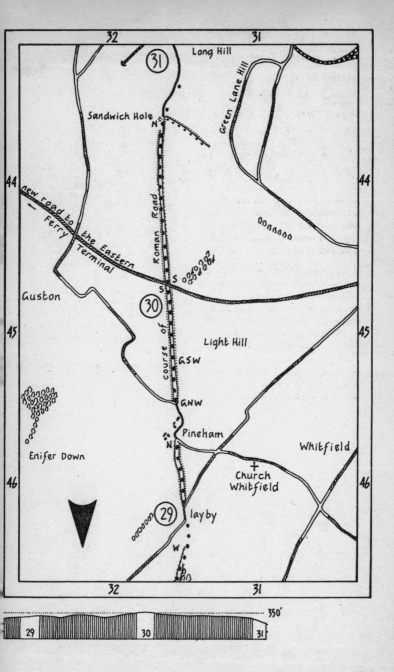

32   31

Long Hill

㉛

Green Lane Hill

Sandwich Hole

N

44   44

new road to the Eastern
Ferry Terminal

Roman Road

Guston

S

S

㉚

course of

45   45

Light Hill

GSW

GNW

N

Pineham

Whitfield

Enifer Down

✝
Church
Whitfield

46   46

㉙   lay by

W

32   31

350'

29   30   31

C12. Dover

$1\frac{1}{4}$ miles
Maps: 1:25000 sheet TR34; 1:50000 sheet 179

East-bound: Follow the road across the railway to the cemetery, bear right, continue downhill to the road junction and then follow the main road into Dover.

West-bound: Leave Dover along the Maison Dieu Road, turn right along Frith Road, cross over at the junction with Connaught Road and Barton Road to follow a minor road to the cemetery. Fork left and follow the road.

Dover (population 35,000) has a Tourist Information Centre at Townwall Street (tel. Dover 205108) and at the Town Hall, High Street (tel. Dover 206941). It is an excellent transport centre with good bus and rail services to London and most parts of Kent. Early closing day is Wednesday. (*For a description of Dover see p. 145.*)

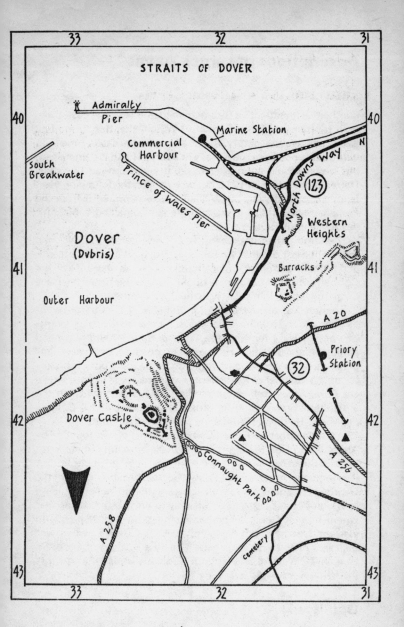

Descriptions of Larger Towns

Farnham

Farnham is an attractive Georgian market town. The castle was built by Henry of Blois, Bishop of Winchester, during the first half of the twelfth century. It was an adulterine castle (one built without licence from the King) and Henry II had it demolished, but it was rebuilt soon afterwards. It was captured by Louis, Dauphin of France, in 1216 but was retaken the following year. During the Civil War, Sir William Waller captured it from the Parliamentarians and it was slighted. It remained a bishop's residence until 1956.

The large parish church of St Andrew dates from Norman times but most of what we see now was built in the fourteenth and fifteenth centuries. In the churchyard is the grave of William Cobbett, who was born in the public house which now bears his name but which in his day was the Jolly Farmer.

Cobbett was always a thorn in the side of the authorities as he championed reforms of all kinds. He started life as a ploughboy and in 1802 founded the *Political Register* and published parliamentary debates. He was sentenced to two years' imprisonment for denouncing flogging in the army but eventually became a Member of Parliament. Two of his most famous works are *Rural Rides*, still worth reading for his comments on the agricultural practices in the British countryside, and *A Cottage Economy*. He died at Normandy Farm near Guildford.

In Castle Street are some Elizabethan almshouses, founded by Andrew Windsor, for 'eight poor honest impotent old persons'. In West Street can be seen Vernon House, now the public library. It is actually much older than it looks, because behind the Georgian façade is a sixteenth-century timber-framed building in which Charles I stayed on his way to his trial in London and where he met General Thomas Harris, who signed his death warrant. Nearby is the museum, in Wilmer House, which was built in 1718. It was once Miss Wilmer's Boarding School for Girls. At 10 West Street was born Augustus Toplady, who wrote the hymn *Rock of Ages*.

Guildford

There is much for the visitor to see in Guildford, which was the ancient capital of Surrey. The cobbled High Street, one of the most attractive in the south of England, climbs steeply up from the river. From the seventeenth-century Guildhall hangs the famous clock, which was made some time during the 1560s, although the case itself dates from 1683. Above the Guildhall, on the same side of the street, is Guildford House, built in 1660 for a wealthy merchant and now an exhibition centre. Near the top of the High Street is the Hospital of the Holy Trinity, built as an almshouse by George Abbot, Archbishop of Canterbury, in the early part of the seventeenth century. Opposite is the church of Holy Trinity, which was rebuilt in the eighteenth century and contains the tomb of Archbishop Abbot and the chantry of Sir Richard Weston of Sutton Place, which is believed to be the last chantry built in England. In Quarry Street, just off the bottom of the High Street, is the church of St Mary, which has a Saxon tower and much Norman work. Part of the east end was demolished at the request of the Prince Regent to allow the road to be widened. Nearby are the remains of the castle, which was built by Henry II probably on the site of an earlier Saxon castle. Lewis Carroll died at the Chestnuts in Castle Hill in 1898. Guildford has a modern cathedral, which was begun in 1936 and completed in 1961, on Stag Hill near the University of Surrey.

Rochester

The view from the Medway bridge, although striking, gives an impression of an industrial city. But Rochester is much more than a collection of factories; it has always been an important river crossing and is the lowest point at which the Medway could be bridged. The Romans and the Saxons had castles here and from the latter, Hrofe-Caestre, is derived the name Rochester. The Christian church was founded here in AD 604 by St Augustine, William the Conqueror built a castle and Gundulph, the Norman Archbishop of Canterbury, founded a monastery. The town is on the line of the main road from London to Canterbury and Bridge Chapel was built for pilgrims in 1397, though subsequently it has been much restored. There are still some traces of the town walls. The Norman keep dominates the town and has massive walls 13 ft thick with passages inside some of them. The town has many associations with Dickens, who lived nearby at Gad's Hill. Scenes from *Pickwick Papers* and *Great Expectations* were set at the Bull Hotel and Mr Jingle described Rochester as: 'Ah, fine place, glorious pile – frowning walls – tottering arches – dark nooks – crumbling staircases – old cathedral, too – earthy smell – pilgrims' feet worn away the old steps – little Saxon doors – fine old place – old legends, too – strange stories – capital.'

The cathedral itself is small, but full of interest as it contains examples of all architectural styles from the eleventh to the twentieth century. St Augustine founded the first cathedral here, but that was sacked by the Danes and only traces remain. Gundulph began a new cathedral in 1077, of which the crypt and the south aisle of the nave remain. The fabric of the building has suffered over the years. It was badly damaged by two separate fires in the twelfth century, looted on several occasions by the Danes and sundry other vandals, including the local townspeople, damaged by Cromwell's soldiers and over-restored by the Victorians.

Canterbury

There is so much to see in Canterbury, one of the most interest-ing cities in England, that only a brief summary can be given here. In particular, visitors to the cathedral are urged to buy the excellent guide on sale at the bookstall.

The city is built on the Stour and has been of great strategic importance from the earliest time. The Romans called it Duro-vernum Cantiacorum, which means the Kentish men's fort on the marsh, which seems to indicate that there was an Iron Age settlement here. There certainly was at Bigbury, $2\frac{1}{2}$ miles west of the city, but it may be that there was another site which the Romans built over to construct their garrison town. Duro-vernum was the junction of important roads from Londinium (London) to the ports of Rutupiae (Richborough), Dubris (Dover) and Portus Lemanus (Lympne) and was thus one of the important gateways into England from Rome and Gaul. Through it marched the legions which policed the country as far north as the Roman Wall on the Scottish border and to accommodate them were constructed barracks and an amphitheatre.

The Saxons renamed Canterbury Cantwarabyring (the fort-ress of the men of Kent) and by A D 560 it was the capital of the Saxon kingdom of Kent. King Ethelbert had a Frankish wife who was a Christian and she welcomed St Augustine, who arrived from Rome to convert England in 597. He took over the existing Christian church of St Martin, made Canterbury the centre of his missionary activities and founded the see. In addition to St

Thomas à Becket, two other Archbishops of Canterbury were canonized. The first was St Dunstan, who reformed the English Church, established the Benedictine rule in England and died in 988. The second was St Alphege, a relation of St Dunstan, who became Archbishop in 1005 and was martyred by the Danes because he refused to pay them a ransom for his release from captivity.

The Normans built a castle (the keep can be seen just off Mercery Lane) and rebuilt the cathedral, which had been sacked by the Danes in 1067. Only the crypt of this cathedral now remains, as much of it was destroyed by fire in 1174, only 44 years after it was consecrated. Money poured in from pilgrims and others visiting the shrine of St Thomas and rebuilding began in the following year. In 1220, Becket's remains were transferred to a magnificent new shrine which was completely destroyed during the Reformation. More rebuilding took place in the fourteenth century and one hundred years later was added Bell Harry Tower.

Like all great Gothic cathedrals, the beauty and magnificence of the building is breathtaking and it would take many visits to know and understand the many treasures that are on display. There is much glorious stained glass which survived the bombing and some magnificent tombs, including those of the Black Prince, Archbishop Chichele, Lady Margaret Holland and her two husbands John Beaufort, the Earl of Somerset, and Thomas Plantagenet, the son of Henry IV.

The walls of the city were built in the fourteenth century as was the fine Westgate, now a museum. Henry II walked barefoot and in sackcloth through this gate on his way to be scourged and do penance for the murder of Becket. In the gardens near the city walls is a monument to Christopher Marlowe, who was born in the city and baptized at St George's church, which was destroyed by German bombing during the war. Just off Longport, in North Holmes Road on the route out of Canterbury on the way to Patrixbourne, is the church given to St Augustine where King Ethelbert was baptized. We know that St Martin's was already built when St Augustine landed in 597, which makes it the oldest church in England.

Dover

Dover, the old Roman Dubris, is situated in a splendid position. Although to a historian it is one of the most interesting towns in England, it must be admitted that it is not a particularly attractive place. It suffered much from bombing and shelling during the war and most of the rebuilding is undistinguished. The castle, which is superbly sited overlooking the town, was built in the last quarter of the twelfth century by Henry II and has been occupied by the military ever since. The keep contains two chapels and has a 250-ft well which was dug to keep the garrison supplied with drinking water. In 1803 the curtain walls were lowered to make gun platforms to provide defences against invasion by the French. It also contains the impressive remains of the pharos, or lighthouse, which was built by the Romans to assist navigation. Originally it was about 100 ft high although only some 40 ft now remains and some of this is not Roman work. The Saxons used it as a bell tower for the little church of St Mary in Castro, a tenth-century cruciform church with an aisle-less nave.

There are a number of interesting buildings in the town itself. In the High Street is the Maison Dieu Hall, which was built at the beginning of the thirteenth century as a hostel for pilgrims and was used by those going to Canterbury, Rome, the Holy Land and Compostela. It was closed when pilgrimages ceased at the Reformation and is now the town museum. Next door is Maison Dieu House, which was built in 1665 and now contains the public library. Nearby, in Priory Road, can be seen St Edmund's Chapel, consecrated by St Richard of Chichester in 1253. It is very small and at some stage of its history became lost. It was rediscovered just before the last war when it had become a blacksmith's shop. The premises were acquired by the Catholic Church and the chapel has been restored and re-dedicated.

During the excavation of the car park in 1970 a Roman painted house was discovered in New Street and this has been preserved in the specially constructed exhibition. It is probably the finest example of a painted house of the period north of the Alps.

Dover college incorporates parts of the old Benedictine Priory of St Martin. The refectory is one of the best examples of a Norman secular building left in the country.

List of Accommodation

This list of accommodation is arranged in geographical order from west (Farnham) to east (Dover). The nearest mile number on the maps is shown in the entry together with a grid reference where this seems appropriate.

Guildford (1 mile north of the Path between mile 10 and 11)
  Newman's Guest House, 24 Waterden Road, GU1 2AY, tel. (0483) 60558
  L. Parsons, Greyfriars, 9 Castle Hill, GU1 3SX, tel. (0483) 61795

Albury (1 mile south of the Path at mile 15)
  Edgeley Caravan and Camping Park (grid reference TQ 062471)
  Mrs D. Jeorrett, Fairlee, Farley Green, Guildford GU5 9DN, tel. Shere (048 641) 2143

Shere (1 mile south of the Path at mile 16)
  Mrs M. James, Manor Cottage, GU5 9JE, tel. (048 641) 2979

Gomshall (1 mile south of the Path at mile 18)
  Mrs M. Pickles, Road Down Chase, Colekitchen Lane, GU5 9QB, tel. Shere (048641) 2408

Dorking (1 mile south of the Path between miles 23 and 24)
  Mrs E. Dawson, 74 Chalkpit Lane, RH4 1HT, tel. (0306) 889199
  Star and Garter Hotel, Station Approach, RH4 1TF, tel. (0306) 882820

Box Hill (mile 25)
  Byways Camping and Caravan Site, Box Hill Road, Tadworth (just off Path)

Reigate (1 mile south of the Path between miles 30 and 31)
  Cranleigh Hotel, West Street, RH2 9BL, tel. (073 72) 43468
  Norfolk Lodge Hotel, 23–25 London Road, RH2 9DY, tel. (073 72) 48702

Redhill (1 mile south of the Path at mile 31)

Brompton Guest House, 6 Crossland Road, RH1 4AN, tel. (0737) 65613

The Ivy House, Nutfield Road, RH1 4ED, tel. (0737) 66701

Wrotham ($\frac{1}{2}$ mile north of the Path at mile 59)

Thriftwood Farm Camping Site, Plaxdale Green Road (grid reference TQ 598608)

Harrietsham (mile 88)

Mrs M. Bottle, Dial House, East Street, ME17 1HJ, tel. Maidstone (0622) 859622

Charing ($\frac{1}{2}$ mile south of the Path between miles 94 and 95)

West Leacon Farm (bed and breakfast), Westwell Leacon, TN27 0EL, tel. Charing (023 371) 3062 (grid reference TQ 954474)

Westwell ($\frac{1}{2}$ mile north of the Path at mile 96)

Camping and bed and breakfast available at Dean Court, Challock Lane, tel. Charing (023 371) 2924 (grid reference TQ 990486)

Kennington ($1\frac{1}{4}$ miles south of the Path at mile 99)

Croft Hotel, Canterbury Road, tel. Ashford (0233) 22140

Downs View Hotel, Willesborough Road, tel. (0233) 21953

Wye (mile 100)

New Flying Horse Inn, Upper Bridge Street, tel. (0233) 812297

Folkestone (1 mile south of the Path at mile 117)

Folkestone is a holiday resort with a great deal of accommodation which is too plentiful to list. The following campsites lie near the Path:

Sunny Bank Farm, Gibraltar Lane, Hawkinge ($\frac{1}{2}$ mile north of Path at grid reference TR 211387)

Little Switzerland Camping Site, The Warren Camping Site (both these sites are on the beach near mile 119)

Dover

The bed and breakfast accommodation is too plentiful to list. There is a campsite near mile 121 at the Plough Inn on the A20.

Accommodation on the Canterbury Loop

Chilham (mile 6)

Pope Street Farmhouse, tel. (022 776) 226 (1 mile south-east of the Path between miles 4 and 5)

Mrs J. Olsen, Manyora House, Hambrook Close, tel. (022 776) 768

Canterbury (mile 13)

    The bed and breakfast accommodation is too plentiful to list.

    St Martin's Camping Site, Bekesbourne Lane (1 mile north of Path, just off the A257 at grid reference TR 173575)

Womenswold (mile 21)

    Woodpeckers Country Hotel, tel. Barham (022 782) 319

Coldred (mile 25)

    Coldred Court Farm, tel. Shepherdswell (0304) 830816 (on Path)

Index of Place Names

Index of Place Names

Index of Place Names

Find out more about Penguin Books

The Penguin Footpath Guides

H. D. Westacott
Mapped by Hugh Richards

The Brecon Beacons National Park
The Cornwall South Coast Path
Dartmoor for Walkers and Riders
The Devon South Coast Path
The Dorset Coast Path
The Ridgeway Path
The Somerset and North Devon Coast Path
The South Downs Way

also by H. D. Westacott in Penguins

The Walker's Handbook
Second Enlarged Edition

Maps, tents, clothes, rights of way, National Parks, the law, hostels, farmers, gamekeepers, shoes, boots, safety and first aid – all you need to know to walk safely and happily, whether you take the low road or the high road. This new and enlarged edition also includes extra chapters on challenge walks and walking abroad.

More Penguins for Walkers

First Aid for Hill Walkers and Climbers
Jane Renouf and Stewart Hulse

This practical, sensible and long-needed manual will slip easily into a pocket or rucksack. It has been compiled with the aid of rescuers and experienced climbers and walkers from all over Britain. While not intended as a substitute for a first-aid course, it tells you how to deal with accidents on the mountainside and how to set about getting help in the most efficient and least panicky way: and, for easy reference the authors list the different accidents and illnesses in alphabetical order, ranging from asthma to vertigo.

A Hitch-hiker's Guide to Great Britain
Ken Lussey
Illustrated by Reg Piggott

Whether you're a beginner or an expert, this handbook provides the essential information to enable you to hitch safely and enjoyably from A to B, with the minimum of time, trouble and expense. Dividing Britain into ten regions for easy reference, the guide features

● maps to show the best pick-up points on motorway junctions and A roads, rated according to a carefully devised grading system

● large-scale maps giving hitching-ratings at spots in city and town centres throughout Britain

● information on equipment, motorways and camping, and many more useful hints